C000104505

'JUBILEES' AND 'JUBBLYS'

A trainspotter's story
Part 1: Spring 1959 to August 1962

Stewart Warrington

Silver Link Publishing Ltd

First published in 2014

British Library Cataloguing in Publication Data

A catalogue record for this book is available from the British Library.

ISBN 978 1 85794 444 0

Silver Link Publishing Ltd
The Trundle
Ringstead Road
Great Addington
Kettering
Northants NN14 4BW

Tel/Fax: 01536 330588
email: sales@nostalgiacollection.com
Website: www.nostalgiacollection.com

Printed and bound in the Czech Republic

Front cover: 'Jubilee' 4-6-0 No 45674 *Duncan* storms out of Derby on a Hinckley to Blackpool special. *Tony Moore*

CONTENTS

PREFACE

First, an apology to anyone of a technical disposition who may be interested in railways: thanks for looking, but sadly this book is not for you. However, if you are a trainspotter who enjoyed collecting numbers, especially in those wonderful days of steam, then welcome aboard for a journey through its pages, during which I hope you will be reminded of some of the joys of the hobby we shared.

Harry Usmar/D. J. Hucknall collection

'JUBILEES' AND 'JUBBLYS'

So, yes, despite the stigma associated with the hobby, I'm proud to admit that I'm a trainspotter, and this is a book recording those observations I made around 50 years ago chasing steam. If any mistakes are discovered please accept my apologies; put them down to all that dashing around those dimly lit engine sheds scribbling down loco numbers as fast as you could, especially when, dare I say, you were there sometimes without permission.

Regarding the 'numbers' they all come from some very tatty old record books I've managed to save through the years, despite house moves and the occasional clear-outs that always make you feel better when you cast the past away. Thank goodness I didn't, and after so many years I'm still able to glance through their pages, helping to transport me back in time, becoming 13 years old again about to underline my cops in the Ian Allan *abc* after a Sunday shed bash.

In writing my book one of the things I've enjoyed has been the lively discussions with my old trainspotting friends. Their accounts as to what happened on our days out, especially from my lifelong friend 'Big Stu', have been invaluable, together with the information and pictures supplied by Tony Moore, who I bumped into at a local watering hole, having not seen him for 50 years!

Finally many thanks to my dear wife Carolyn, who has helped check these words, not numbers, and says she enjoyed reading my story, despite all the young ladies mentioned.

Here's hoping you enjoy it too.

Stewart Warrington
Trainspotter

'On a Club trip today, Mum – 15 sheds and a works to visit, so may be late home tonight.'

Foreword

By David Allan,
Chairman, Ian Allan Publishing Ltd

Locospotting is still alive and well and locospotters can still be seen at many stations and in great numbers at places like Doncaster, Reading, Crewe and York, but it is not the trainspotter of the 1940s that we now see. The locospotters today are very often in late middle age and equipped with electronic and even digital equipment to assist them in their hobby.

Locospotters in the 1940s, '50s and '60s were a less technical bunch, armed with a range of different-coloured ball points and pencils, usually of school age dressed in school uniform and taking photographs and numbers from a pre-health-and-safety-era vantage point.

Stewart Warrington's book took me back to the days when I was a trainspotter in the Sixties – not so much a trainspotter's story as a blow-by-blow account of his surprise and that of his friends as they discovered more about the railway system.

It is amazing to think that there were half a million trainspotters at one stage who had signed up to become a member of the Ian Allan Locospotters Club; a badge, membership card and pencil were proof that one was a member, but there was also the code of conduct that allowed you to spot numbers from the rail side, and Stewart's book takes you back to those days of excitement and discovery.

The days when most trains were made up of mixed rolling stock and no two locomotives looked the same; when locomotive drivers had star status and were known by thousands by name; when Chief Mechanical Engineers were not only household names but held God-like status among those who worked on the railways.

Every trainspotter had a different way of taking numbers; some would buy two copies of every book, one for taking the number and one for recording it. Some tried to underline every number in their book, while others, such as Rex Kennedy of OPC, spent a lifetime trying to underline every number in his 1962 Combined Volume. Almost every male from the age of 60 will have at some time or another embarked on the hobby of trainspotting, which gave one freedom to travel and an interest just beyond taking numbers, as the hugely successful Shed Allocation books proved.

From a commercial point of view, the introduction of Locospotting books and their success came as a surprise. The first edition, *The ABC of Southern Locomotives*, had a print run of 5,000 and had sold out within a fortnight – and these were in the days where the internet was unheard of. Queues of young boys would be seen outside the Allan household where my father lived with his parents, and by the time all four railway companies had been covered W. H. Smith was taking thousands, all of which were pre-ordered before the new edition had been published.

The spotters' books developed into hardback books on railways and how they were run, rather than the more academic works that had been the staple diet for books on railways before the war, and led to the introduction of railway enthusiasts' special trains being organised throughout the late 1940s and '50s, culminating in the formation of Ian Allan Travel in the early 1960s, headed by a railway enthusiast of the Ffestiniog Railway.

I thoroughly enjoyed reading Stewart's personal trip down Memory Lane.

David Allan
Shepperton, October 2014

1959

'A life-long passion.' Can you remember the moment when the magic began? My moment came in the spring of 1959 at York's wonderful railway station. Having arrived on a school visit to the city, I was stunned by my first view of one of Gresley's streamlined 'A4' 'Pacifics', No 60006 *Sir Ralph Wedgwood*, passing through. I had never seen anything so sleek, powerful, and exciting before. From that moment I was hooked, and immediately became a trainspotter, and 50-odd years later I'm proud to say I still am. I know today trainspotting sounds a bit naff, but back then it was one of the most popular hobbies for us young boys.

What was the attraction? Many reasons: in the late '50s there were thousands of steam locomotives working all over the country, of different shapes, sizes and liveries, some clean, a lot dirty, some with wonderful names, all numbered, some fast, some slow, some new, some old, both familiar or rare, depending on where you happened to live. Add an important ingredient to our young lads' collecting minds – we could gather engine numbers – so no wonder we laid down our books of stamps, cigarette cards, matchboxes, fruit wrappers, birds' eggs, and shells (when on seaside holidays), and became 'spotters'. It was better still if you could share your hobby with your best pals and school mates, as I did with 'Big Stu' Atkinson (I was known as 'Little Stew'), Stanley Lance Richardson, Colin Field, and Mick Harby. We were all young lads of 12 or 13 growing up in a very different time.

Our new interest caught our imaginations, and broadened our horizons through travel, the Ian Allan *abc* books, Tizer drinks, Mars bars, Wagon Wheels and, of course, Ice Jubblys. Our home city of Leicester was then blessed with two main railway lines – the Midland and the Great Central – offering plenty of variety for a young trainspotter. We also had the 'Birdcage', which provided a perfect viewing spot for us overlooking the Midland shed yards, and roundhouse. It was reached by an elevated alleyway overlooking the main line north of London Road station, which opened out onto Hutchinson Walk, with one side offering a view through its railings, hence its nickname.

One of the big things about growing up in the late 1950s was the freedom we enjoyed by obtaining bicycles. None of our parents had cars, so a bike was a must; mine was a Raleigh Palm Beach, with a blue and white frame, Sturmey Archer three-speed gears, and Dynohub lighting. Being mobile in the early days of our hobby made all the difference and, with visits every weekend and most days during the school holidays, the 'Birdcage' soon became our second home. The allocation of steam engines to Leicester shed (15C), although large, was mainly made up of mixed-traffic and freight locomotives. Early memories from our visits were of a couple of stored old Midland 4-4-0s parked on a

The view of the Midland shed at Leicester from the 'Birdcage' area.
Horace A. Gamble

line down below the alleyway, No 40543 being one of them, and, before diesel shunters arrived, watching a busy little station pilot, 0-6-0 No 47203, shunting around the local carriage yards and London Road's platforms. These particular types of tank engine we soon learned were nicknamed 'Jinties' by local enthusiasts.

On the main line we enjoyed collecting the 'Jubilees', 'Scots' and 'Britannias', which powered the express trains; we loved seeing them and never imagined that within a few years they would be replaced by diesel power. I think at this stage of my story I'd better mention that British Railways was beginning to introduce a lot of new diesel locomotives, including multiple units (DMUs), which much to our disgust were replacing steam on local services. Although the collection of main-line diesel numbers was acceptable to us, when it came to spotting DMUs it was not, and our group very early on chose to ignore them, never bothering to record their numbers. We even frowned on other spotters who did – for us they didn't count, which is why my story or records rarely mention DMUs.

By this time we were amongst 950 boys attending our large estate's Secondary Modern school. All of us were encouraged to wear the school uniform, and if your class was lucky enough to be recognised as the smartest group of boys during the week, you were allowed to leave early on Friday afternoons. What's this got to do with train spotting? Well, we often took advantage of this 'perk' to dash off to London Road station to see the southbound 'Palatine' express arriving at Leicester around 4.40pm, then a regular duty for a 'Britannia' 'Pacific'. It was followed around an hour later by the Midland main line's other important train, the 'Thames-Clyde Express', with its 'Jubilee' or 'Royal Scot' in charge. Mentioning our school uniforms, it might surprise you to learn that, as young boys, not only were we smart at school, but usually went trainspotting wearing those uniforms, often with collar and tie, school blazer, and grey flannel trousers; it was only natural then because casual clothes were non-existent, we were too young to wear sports jackets, and the 'Swinging Sixties' fashion was in the future. Our parents often obtained our school uniforms 'on the weekly', and we were under strict orders to ensure they lasted despite us pursuing at times dirty, grimy steam engines.

I mentioned earlier that my home city was blessed with another main line, the Great Central, which I'm sure provided me with my first spotting experience thanks to my Grandfather Dennis, who often took me on walks from his home to the nearby West Bridge area of town, pointing out the trains to me as they passed over the elevated line and bridges into Central station. So, well before I officially started my hobby I'm sure I watched 'A3' 'Pacifics' at work, remembering the name *Enterprise* particularly, and discovering later that the Leicester GC shed had its own allocation of the Gresley 'Pacifics' in the early '50s, including No 60111, suggested I certainly did.

Anyway, I'd like to think it was he who set the seeds to my eventual lifelong interest in steam locomotives. Sadly the 'A3s' had all disappeared back to the Eastern Region by the time we became spotters, but the 'Master Cutler' express from London to Sheffield was still running, often pulled by one of Gresley's 'V2' 2-6-2s, or a Thompson 'B1' 4-6-0, including No 61008 *Kudu*, which was at the time the only named locomotive allocated to either of our Leicester sheds. I think it's fair to say at the beginning that the Great Central line wasn't as glamorous for us boys as the busy Midland route, nor did it offer the same excitement for us. The Midland's far larger stock of express motive power was the main difference, providing us young spotters with different 'namer' cops to be seen virtually every time we ventured down the 'Birdcage'. True, the GC's 9F 2-10-0s on their fast freight trains, called 'Windcutters', were impressive, but to be honest, being freight engines, as young spotters we didn't really appreciate them or the main line until a few years later.

Unlike the Leicester Midland depot, we never had a problem having a look around the Central shed, and it was always nice to see its allocation of 'V2s', Nos 60831/42/63, plus its 'B1s', including of course *Kudu*. I remember that she soon became so familiar to us that the shout of 'Scrap it!' was often the reaction when she appeared. Not by me, of course – I was far too intelligent. As if she knew she wasn't appreciated, she moved away in 1960 to Agecroft, in Manchester, before being based in Scotland in 1963 at Eastfield, Glasgow, finally being withdrawn from Carstairs in December 1966. Funnily enough, although I never saw her at Leicester again, I did catch up with her on my future travels a couple of times over the years, which you will see.

Incidentally, the Great Central engine shed (15E) was situated beside the Grand Union Canal. It may sound strange to

Leicester Central shed in 1963. *Horace A. Gamble/transporttreasuary.co.uk*

relate that on one visit to train-spot there I became a life-saver, but more about that later.

I'm not quite sure when I started to earn a living, but it must have been around then, when I became an evening paperboy for Kenny & Tomlin newsagent's shop in Woodgate, Leicester. I was paid 5 shillings a week for delivering an evening local newspaper, the *Leicester Mercury*, in the Blackbird Road and Anstey Lane area of the city. Not only did I suddenly have money to help fund my spotting hobby, but doing my job also brought me in contact with another railway line that I'd not mentioned yet, the West Bridge line, the former Leicester & Swannington Railway engineered by

I took this photograph of the freight on the West Bridge line, which was not far from the estate where we lived, in the winter of 1961.

I remember as small boys we often placed pennies on the line there to see them flattened by the train. And guess who's kept one of those pennies from all those years ago!

Robert Stephenson. Its single-track line ran from its Leicester terminus near West Bridge through a large allotment area above Fosse Road on its way out of the city to Glenfield, and having climbed quite a steep road called Jean's Drive on my paper round I was often able to watch the early evening coal and oil freight train pulled by an ancient Johnson 2F 0-6-0 in the distance slowly making its way out of the city. Only a couple of daily trains ran on the line, which was freight only, but I loved to see the white exhaust of the little Johnson engine as she went along. It's nice to think that I was able to enjoy a ride on the goods train a few years later.

Now I can't remember who suggested our first spotting away trip from Leicester, but I know it was by train to Nuneaton, where on a hot summer's Saturday we experienced a very busy West Coast Main Line with express after express steam-hauled, only a couple of the new Type 4 English Electric diesels appearing to spoil the day's steam dominance. Sadly my records of the day have been long lost, but I do remember the number of 'Royal Scots' observed was well over the 20 mark, with a large number of 'Jubilees' and 'Patriots' together with a dozen 'Coronation Pacifics', and four or five of the 'Princess' class. It was simply amazing to us young boys to witness the sight of so many express engines, and their famous express trains: the 'Royal Scot', 'Caledonian', 'Shamrock', 'Irish Mail', 'Lakes Express', 'Merseyside Express', 'Red Rose', 'Emerald Isle Express' and 'Mid-Day Scot'.

A few weeks later we caught a Midland Red bus to travel to Grantham for the East Coast Main Line. On hearing that trainspotting on the station was punishable by death (things were exaggerated in those days by fellow spotters) we positioned ourselves north of the station beside a large area of open land, which formed the rail triangle that accessed the nearby 34F locomotive depot. Two memories I retain of the day are of 'A2' 'Pacific' No 60506 *Wolf of Badenoch*, one of the class without smoke deflectors, with its long nameplate positioned high on its front boiler side, making its way light engine around to the shed, and the sky-blue prototype 'Deltic' diesel with its 'speed whiskers' stopping in front of us on a northbound express.

Back to the West Coast, Rugby became our next destination, one of the few times we managed to travel there by rail from London Road station, thanks to Dr Beeching's railway closures a year or so later. Perhaps this was not a bad thing for me as it turned out, after I managed to lose my half-fare train ticket out of the carriage window on the way home. Despite my tearful explanation at the station barrier, I received no sympathy, and was forced to pay for another ticket at Leicester. With no money left, the boys clubbed together to save me and gave me the cash, something Big Stu reminds me of regularly even today, especially when we are at the local! Still it was the day we saw a famous steam engine, No 46100 *Royal Scot*, as it passed northbound on an express. I also noted my first ever Great Western locomotive, a 'Hall' Class 4-6-0, when it passed over the nearby bridge carrying the Great Central main line.

Towards the end of 1959 we joined a local railway club for enthusiasts, the Great Central Railway Society of Leicester. It was a new club started earlier that year by 17-year-old Tony Moore, who lived in Birstall, a suburb of Leicester. We all attended one of the first meetings, which was held at Tony's house, and was so well attended that our school pal Colin Field ended up sitting in the dog's basket. Strange things you remember! When the club became more organised its meetings were held at the Birstall Methodist Church Hall, an ideal venue for us boys, allowing us at the end of evening to take advantage of the nearby local chippy, enjoying a bag of chips before dashing down the 'Birdcage' to see the night's diesel-hauled 'Condor' express freight train passing through London Road around 9.30pm hauled by a pair of 'Metrovick' D5700s, then the very latest in British Railways diesel motive power.

Joining the club proved one of the best decisions we ever made, as organised visits to steam sheds around the country suddenly became available to us, and it wasn't long before we joined the first organised coach outing in January 1960 to five sheds in the Nottingham area on a Sunday, which was always the best day to visit as it tended to produce the largest number of engines present at depots. Sadly none of my records of our spotting that day have survived, but I do remember visiting the very large freight engine depot at Toton (18A), which was stacked out with well over 100 steam freight engines, and the former Great Central sheds at Annesley (16D) and Colwick (40E).

Returning to our own day trips around this time, one of them took us to Birmingham by rail, and although we arrived at New Street station, it was Snow Hill that was our destination, and we soon made our way there hoping to experience Great Western steam locomotives in action for the very first time. We certainly weren't disappointed, observing a procession of the Region's 'Castles' and 'Kings' on expresses, and apart from the dreaded DMUs I'm sure everything we saw, including freight traffic, was steam-hauled. Brought up on Midland 'Jubilees' and 'Royal Scots', what a contrast these wonderful engines were, hauling their 'chocolate and cream' coaching stock; it seemed like we had travelled to a different railway world, all adding to the magic of spotting for us young boys. It certainly was busy, with the route enjoying additional traffic between London and Birmingham at the time because of the West Coast Main Line electrification work.

Another day out saw us travel to London to visit the main-line stations. 'A4' 'Pacific' No 60019 *Bittern* was noted departing from King's Cross, my first Southern Region 'Lord Nelson' 4-6-0, No 30860 *Lord Hawke*, was recorded on a boat train from Southampton at Waterloo, and a 'Duchess' was seen at the old Euston station. Our train back to Leicester was hauled by 'Jubilee' No 45706 *Express*. If I remember correctly, our parents were unhappy about a visit to the capital, so a 'white lie' covered our tracks – we told them we were visiting the Motor Show. Sorry, Mum.

Christmas was always an interesting time for us trainspotters, and I made a point of visiting London Road station during Christmas Eve for a few years. One early steam Christmas present came on 24 December 1959 when, after purchasing my twopenny platform ticket, I discovered the famous No 46100 *Royal Scot* simmering away on a yard track adjacent to Platform 1. I was surprised to see her at Leicester, knowing that she was

'B1' No 61163 at Leicester Belgrave Road station in 1961. *Horace A. Gamble/transporttreasuary.co.uk*

normally at work on the West Coast line, and even more so when she eventually took out a small local train to Nottingham. I remember being tempted to jump aboard for a ride behind her, but, with no ticket, sadly I behaved. Later on, obtaining a copy of the January 1960 *Trains Illustrated*, all was revealed, with a report of the transfer of No 46100 and sister engine No 46157 to Nottingham shed (16A). Her displacement from the West Coast was no doubt due to the introduction of those dreaded diesels (English Electric Type 4s), and perhaps for the first time I began to realise what modernisation meant to steam. Thinking back, further evidence before this was the appearance the previous summer of No D1, the prototype of the Derby Sulzer Type 4s, later known as 'Peaks'. I remember looking at her on a northbound service one evening, thinking, 'Well, at least she's painted in the Brunswick Green livery similar as the "Jubilees" and "Scots".'

Yes, things were changing, and 1959 finished with the news of a diesel Pullman train for the Western Region – a glorified DMU to me. How awful for us steam engine spotters, but of course it was only the beginning. Before my tale enters the 1960s I'd better mention Belgrave Road station, which boasted six platforms and was the gateway to the East Coast holiday resorts for the citizens of Leicester. As a small boy I often journeyed to Skegness and Mablethorpe on day trips from the station with Mum and Dad, and later with my sister Jane. The station was situated just across the road from a school on Abbey Street where the Great Central Club eventually held its meetings, and we would often pop across to discover – nothing. This was a reflection of the fact that passenger traffic was sparse to say the least, with a small amount of freight, and sadly it was closed in September 1962.

1960

Frustrated as I am regarding the loss of my early records, I'm glad to say that with a visit to Rugby on Monday 25 April 1960 I can start to detail what we actually noted, as my log survived. Despite the observation of 12 English Electric Type 4 diesels, steam power was still very much in evidence, with nine 'Royal Scots', six 'Coronations' (known to us as 'Semis') and two 'Princesses' recorded, together with five 'Jubilees'. Interestingly, two very old 0-6-0s, Nos 58201 and 58221, were also noted shunting in the nearby Rugby shed yard. The most vivid memory I have of our visit that day was the sight and sound of one of the 'Princess' locomotives, No 46211 *Queen Maud*, as she took the platform line blowing off a high fountain of steam from her safety valves as she passed through non-stop. It was an awesome show of power, and I felt as if the whole station was shaking.

From this account you will have gathered that we were allowed to stay on the station's platforms to train-spot, a welcome change from the usual reception received elsewhere, and an empty porter's trolley at the end of the platform provided our headquarters for the day. From there in the distance we could also observe the Rugby shed yards, the locomotive testing station, and the Great Central line railway bridge passing over the West Coast tracks, and the numbers of two 'B1s' were recorded thanks to a couple of fellow enthusiasts we met who were equipped with binoculars.

By now having matured into serious spotters, I thought at this stage I'd better mention our hobby's unofficial 'Rules of Engagement' – well, not quite fighting anyone, but being a gentleman, the practice of cribbing an engine sighting when you had not actually seen the locomotive was not acceptable, and reports of rare Scottish engines at Leicester were often met with suspicion and raised eyebrows. Often the claim was soon proven false, and the culprit banished from ever exchanging information with his fellow enthusiasts. Sadly the practice was quite common with some boys as they tried to impress and gain one-upmanship over us decent spotters. Setting this aside, the exchange of genuine information between us was very helpful, and over the years many a dash was made to the 'Birdcage' or Central to catch a surprising visitor.

Sunday 15 May 1960 proved to be a great day for my friends and me as we made our way early that morning to the St Margaret's bus station in Leicester to join the Great Central Society's first organised visit to London and a number of its famous locomotive sheds. Our journey by coach that day also providing us with our first opportunity to travel down the new M1 motorway, which had opened at the end of the previous year. I remember that we were accompanied by a reporter from a local newspaper, who came along to write an article about our trainspotting trip. Thinking back, it seems strange that it was deemed newsworthy at the time, but it was, and the poor chap must have wondered what he had let himself in for after suffering a rather boisterous group of lads all day, which left him complaining about a headache on our journey home.

His article, which appeared in the *Leicester Illustrated Chronicle*, was quite good, and went down well with my parents. Moving on 50 years, during a visit to the Leicester Record Office I was delighted to discover the very article published in the paper, which I reproduce in full:

A DAY OUT WITH THE TRAIN SPOTTERS

When you are thirteen, full of energy, and with a passion for train-spotting, there is no better way to spend Sunday than dashing around the loco sheds of North London.

You meet – as did forty youthful members of the Leicester Great Central Railway Society last Sunday at St Margaret's bus station at 7.30am – and head for the M1 in a fast modern coach.

By coach? 'I know it sounds like treachery, but there are often no trains on Sunday,' explained Roger Holmes, 18, the Society's

Treasurer. Nor any convenient station, for the spotters' main hunting grounds are out-of-the-way loco sheds, not passenger stations.

Most of them on the coach – in fact most of the Society's 70-odd members – were schoolboys of 12 to 15. The Society was founded last October, 'to encourage interest in all aspects of railways'.

'We study many different subjects: signalling systems, timetable planning, railway history, and the mechanical side of it,' says Secretary Tony Moore, 17.

But needless to say, the main interest of 12 to 15-year-olds is loco-spotting ('not train-spotting please'), that is gathering the numbers of locomotives.

'Bibles' On Board

Everyone on the coach had his 'loco-spotters Bible', a small handbook with numbered lists of every locomotive running on British Railways, 'spotted' numbers neatly underscored.

Sunday's trip, a tour of loco sheds in North London, was the sixth and most ambitious organised by the Society. 'British Railways are most co-operative,' says Roger Holmes. 'They let us have the run of the sheds, and sometimes give us a guide.'

Southall was the first stop. The loco-spotters piled out of the coach, ran across a footpath and along a cinder path, and plunged joyfully into the smoky sheds.

Exciting Old 'Uns

Notebooks in hand, they darted in and out among the huge, black, softly hissing locomotives, and then swarmed round the yard in search of new numbers, neatly dodging shunting engines. The older steam engines came in for most attention. 'They're gradually being replaced by diesels, which are much less exciting,' one knowledgeable 14-year-old explained.

'Did you see those old Great Western rail-cars?' asked another. 'Terrific shed!' exclaimed a third. 'I got 70 cops.' (A cop is a number seen for the first time.)

Flood of Questions

At Willesden the Shed Master supplied a guide, a patient slow-speaking fireman, who led the boys in a straggling line between long rows of locomotives and answered a flood of technical questions. Willesden produced a splendid bag of more than a hundred numbers.

Old Oak Common was even better. One energetic youngster, 13-year-old Michael Harby, notched 126. And one group spent ten ecstatic minutes in the cab of *County of Brecknock*, delving into the mysteries of her gears, pressure gauges, regulator, and dampers.

'I can't understand you lads,' said the veteran railwayman who showed them round. 'You're mad on trains, yet none of you want to work on the railways.'

A chorus of young voices told him why. 'The money's no good. It's a dirty underpaid job.'

Neasden shed was polished off in ten minutes. Cricklewood in twenty, and Camden, one of the dirtiest, grimiest spots in London, in fifteen, by the indefatigably scribbling loco-spotters.

Six-Hour Slog

They pressed on unflagging to Kentish Town ('Disappointing – we've seen a lot of these at Leicester'), and Hornsey, making eight depots in all.

Then they set off home. They had spent six hours slogging round dirty, smoky loco shed yards in the drab industrial suburbs of London – not everyone's idea of a day out. But to the loco-spotters, it had been worth it. Most of them had added between five and six hundred numbers to their collections.

'Not a bad day's work,' commented one youngster, falling into a blissful sleep as the coach sped along the M1.

Of course, a trip to London was very exciting from the young trainspotter's perspective, providing us with our first opportunity to visit some of the famous London sheds, with Old Oak Common and Camden certainly living up to all expectations, as you will see from my list of the motive power we observed at two of the sheds visited.

Old Oak Common (81A), 15 May 1960	
Class	**Number/Name**
BR Type 4	D809 *Champion*
Diesel shunters	D3512, D3599, D3600, D3601, D3604, D3632
4-6-0 'County'	1007 *County of Brecknock*
0-6-0PT '1500'	1507
2-8-0 '4700'	4708
2-6-2T '5100'	4153

4-6-0 'Hall'	4945 *Milligan Hall*, 5918 *Walton Hall*, 5929 *Hanham Hall*, 5934 *Kneller Hall*, 5958 *Knolton Hall*, 5986 *Arbury Hall*, 6910 *Gossington Hall*
4-6-0 'Modified Hall'	6959 *Peatling Hall*, 6961 *Stedham Hall*, 7902 *Eaton Mascot Hall*
4-6-0 'Castle'	4074 *Caldicot Castle*, 4075 *Cardiff Castle*, 4082 *Windsor Castle*, 5029 *Nunney Castle*, 5034 *Corfe Castle*, 5040 *Stokesay Castle*, 5049 *Earl of Plymouth*, 5052 *Earl of Radnor*, 5066 *Sir Felix Pole*, 5077 *Fairey Battle*, 5087 *Tintern Abbey*, 7001 *Sir James Milne*, 7010 *Avondale Castle*, 7017 *G. J. Churchward*, 7020 *Gloucester Castle*, 7030 *Cranbrook Castle*, 7036 *Taunton Castle*
0-6-0PT '5700'	3648, 3658, 4615, 8754, 8762, 8763, 8765, 8767, 8768, 8770, 8771, 8772, 8775, 9658, 9702, 9706, 9784
4-6-0 'King'	6003 *King George IV*, 6009 *King Charles II*, 6010 *King Charles I*, 6013 *King Henry VIII*, 6015 *King Richard III*, 6020 *King Henry IV*, 6021 *King Richard II*, 6024 *King Edward I*, 6026 *King John*
2-6-2T '6100'	6100, 6108, 6117, 6120, 6121, 6145, 6157
0-6-0PT '9400'	8459, 9418, 9423, 9479,
4-6-0 Class 5	44710
2-8-0 8F	48431, 48450
2-8-0 'WD'	90639, 90661
2-10-0 BR 9F	92211, 92240, 92244, 92245, 92247

Camden (1B), 15 May 1960	
Class	**Number/Name**
4-6-0 Class 5	45249
4-6-0 'Patriot'	45512 *Bunsen*
4-6-0 'Jubilee'	45554 *Ontario*, 45560 *Prince Edward Island*, 45574 *India*, 45584 *North West Frontier*, 45696 *Arethusa*
4-6-0 'Royal Scot'	46101 *Royal Scots Grey*, 46122 *Royal Ulster Riflemen*, 46143 *South Staffordshire Regiment*, 46144 *Honourable Artillery Company*, 46153 *The Royal Dragoon*, 46167 *The Hertfordshire Regiment*
4-6-2 'Princess Royal'	46207 *Princess Arthur of Connaught*
4-6-2 'Princess Coronation'	46225 *Duchess of Gloucester*, 46228 *Duchess of Rutland*, 46229 *Duchess of Hamilton*, 46242 *City of Glasgow*, 46247 *City of Liverpool*, 46249 *City of Sheffield*, 46250 *City of Litchfield*
4-6-2 'Britannia'	70046 *Anzac*
BR Type 4	D4 *Great Cable*, D7 *Ingleborough*
EE Type 4	D233, D269
BR Type 2	D5078
EE Type 1	D8037, D8039

From the rest of the sheds visited I remember Southall (81C) being home to a number of old Great Western railcars, certainly more attractive than DMUs, and Willesden having an allocation of 100 locomotives, including six 'Jubilees' and four 'Patriots'. Cricklewood and Kentish Town sheds, servicing our Midland main line, were disappointing, containing very few 'cops' for us, and Hornsey, which was to change to a diesel depot quite soon afterwards, was still a steam shed with 27 of the 'J50' tank engines on view.

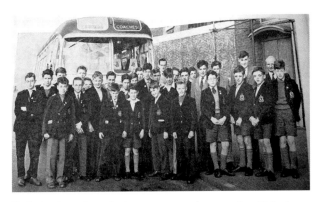

So let's take a closer look at our party photograph, which shows very clearly what I meant about trainspotting in our school uniforms, not to mention short trousers! I'm second from the left on the front row; behind me, with half his head showing, is 'Big Stu' Atkinson, right of me is Stanley Lance Richardson, next to him Mick Harby, whose life I was to save on another adventure, and on his right is Colin Field. Our Club Secretary, Tony Moore, is the tall chap second from right on the back row. I'm reliably informed that the coach, which was new, was operated by Lester Brothers, which I understand is still in business more than 50 years later.

Thinking back to these great trainspotting shed visits, because I was so excited I was never able to sleep the night before, and I remember looking regularly at my wind-up alarm clock, willing the hours to pass by quickly. Often with a very early start, it was up to me to get myself up while my family still slept, leaving the house often before 6.30am, usually collecting Colin Field on the way, to walk the mile or so to Big Stu's house, to meet up with him and Stan, who lived close by. Big Stu, by the way, was spoiled – not only did his parents get him up on these mornings, but he also enjoyed the luxury of a cooked breakfast, and I remember the smell of bacon, eggs and tomatoes filling his kitchen as we collected him.

Our usual coach pick-up point then was outside the Frears

biscuit factory on Woodgate in Leicester, and we would wind our way down the hill from our New Parks estate, through the Fosse Road allotments, and over the Leicester-Swannington single line, admiring the old Midland Railway warning signs on the path rail crossing, which was situated in a very quiet area well away from any houses and surrounded by allotments. Strange to relate, it never occurred to any of us at the time to spirit them away, or that they were of any value. How things were to change, because they certainly would have been treasured mounted on a wall in my home.

This missed opportunity takes me nicely to the August Derby Works Open Day. This annual event attracted a huge number of trainspotters, allowing them to go round the large works to see steam engines being repaired and new diesels being built, and providing an opportunity for the railway souvenir collectors amongst them to have a field day. It's a fact that on the day the works were relieved of many railway items by the hordes as they climbed all over the locomotives present, with many a spanner in use, including the one captured in use by a certain 'Mr Osbourne' all those years ago.

Caught in the act! Thankfully he is not one of 'the boys', so I can include the picture with a clear conscience.

Climbing on locomotives was another thing, as seen during the 1960 Open Day. Health & Safety please look away!

Sorry, I've just remembered, I did relieve the cab of 'Deltic' *Pinza* of a switch cover indicating engine fire as it sat on the scrap line at Doncaster Works. She and a long line of her sisters stood there withdrawn from service on a very grey Sunday in January 1982, a very sad sight. Looking back, I'm so pleased I didn't see many of Gresley's 'Pacifics' at the end of their working life in similar fashion.

Our next Great Central Railway Society trip was to the Bristol area sheds in June, the cost of which was 18s 6d, which we all agreed was worth every penny as it gave us our first opportunity to spot GW steam locomotives in large numbers at Bristol, Worcester, Gloucester and Hereford sheds, as well as enjoying a taste of the Somerset & Dorset line at Bath Green Park shed (82F). A total of ten sheds were visited, including Bristol Bath Road (82A), which was situated quite close to Temple Meads station; this proved to be my only visit there in steam days, as it was closed a few months later and became one of the first to be converted to a diesel depot.

Bristol Bath Road (82A), 12 June 1960	
Class	**Number/Name**
4-6-0 'County'	1028 *County of Warwick*
0-4-0T '1101'	1104
0-4-2T '1400'	1410, 1412
4-4-0 'City'	3440 *City of Truro*
2-6-2T '4500'	5529, 5551
2-8-0 '4700'	4706
4-6-0 'Hall'	4906 *Bradfield Hall*, 4922 *Enville Hall*, 4953 *Pitchford Hall*, 5906 *Lawton Hall*, 5912 *Queen's Hall*, 5950 *Wardley Hall*, 5967 *Bickmarsh Hall*, 5980 *Dingley Hall*, 6915 *Mursley Hall*, 6924 *Grantley Hall* 6925 *Hackness Hall*
4-6-0 'Modified Hall'	6981 *Marbury Hall*, 6983 *Otterington Hall*, 6992 *Arborfield Hall*
2-6-2T '5100'	5104
0-6-0PT '5700'	3604, 3748, 4606, 9626
4-6-0 'Castle'	4077 *Chepstow Castle*, 4083 *Abbotsbury Castle*, 5041 *Tiverton Castle*, 5073 *Blenheim*, 5096 *Bridgewater Castle*, 7003 *Elmley Castle*
4-6-0 'Grange'	6814 *Enborne Grange*, 6847 *Tidmarsh Grange*
0-6-0PT '9400'	8481, 8486, 9481
2-6-2T Class 2	41202, 41249
2-6-2T BR Class 3	82007, 82009, 82028, 82032, 82033, 82035, 82037, 82040, 82042
2-6-2T BR Class 2	84004

It was, I remember, a lovely summer's day during which, having visited a couple of the city's locomotive depots, we enjoyed a short diversion when our coach dropped us off close to the famous Clifton Suspension Bridge, giving us time to stroll across and take in the view. On a tablet mounted next to the bridge entrance was recorded the story of the lady aged 23 who threw herself off the bridge in 1885, but survived the 234-foot fall thanks to her petticoats, which acted like a parachute and slowed down her descent, saving her life. Why mention this? Well, many, many years later yours truly got interested in researching my family tree, and discovered that the young lady in question, Sarah Headley, having survived the fall, later married into my grandmother's branch of the family, the Lanes, and lived to be 83. What's this got to do with railways, you may wonder? Well, there is a railway theme to my story, because she had tried to commit suicide shortly after being jilted by her boyfriend, who was none other than a Great Western Railway porter, so I hope you agree that I haven't moved too far away from writing about my hobby!

By now really enjoying the hobby, I became a regular reader of the monthly Ian Allan *Trains Illustrated* magazine, which was a must for trainspotters. It provided articles and news around the various railway regions, and compiled readers' sightings and locomotive stock changes, which covered withdrawals and transfers between sheds. Steam was featured throughout, and its performance recorded in the 'Locomotive Running Past and Present' section. Add the photographs it featured, and yours truly spent many a breakfast time with my head buried in its pages, studying the latest news.

I had purchased my first copy for 2 shillings in August 1959, from our estate's local newsagent, and remember being thrilled to read it, despite some of its content relating to the modernising of the railways, which I ignored, or, if technical, simply did not understand. I'm sure I ignored the 'Putting over Modernisation' article in the July 1960 edition, which reported that by the end of 1961 BR steam locomotives should be reduced to around 10,700 in number, with little steam surviving on some routes including

This photograph of our party going round St Phillip's Marsh shed (82B) on 12 June 1960 captures both 'Big Stu' (facing the camera) and me on the right-hand side busy scribbling down the precious numbers of the 60-plus engines found on shed.

the East Coast Main Line, where it would be reduced to freight traffic only. A chart also gave details of main-line diesels in service or ordered, which totalled 1,653, of which around 550 were already in service. Things were changing very quickly, a fact that again, perhaps because of our ages, we didn't grasp or appreciate. We loved the magic of steam, and couldn't imagine that time was running out for the majestic express locomotives that were still hauling the most important trains in every town or city we visited.

On reflection, 1960 was for me steam's swan-song, after which the march of progress became more obvious even to us who chose to ignore it. Only years later can one appreciate just how good it was for us, with the concept of withdrawal or scrapping of our favourite engines something we did not dream could happen. Perhaps it reflected the attitude of youngsters towards their heroes such as Superman and Flash Gordon – ours were the steam giants, the Gresley 'A4s', Stanier 'Pacifics', Western

'Castles' and 'Kings', etc, and we didn't want to lose them.

And now to something I mentioned earlier that brought so much enjoyment to us youngsters when out enjoying train-spotting. Yes – the Ice Jubbly. This was a large orange-flavoured frozen ice pyramid costing fourpence that you sucked on for hours; with all the juice consumed, you were left with a solid block of ice, often used in a Jubbly-throwing contest, Big Stu being an easy target. Great fun by the lineside!

The thrill of seeing locomotives for the first time was all the more enjoyable when the time came to check your list of notes and identify those 'cops', and my old record books suggested that on the London trip featured earlier I notched up 348 of them out of a total of 383 engines seen, and on the Bristol outing 324 out of 380. Having completed that task, you then moved on to record their sightings in your trainspotting bible, the Ian Allan *abc of*

British Railways Locomotives, Combined Volume. In this you would underline each new engine number spotted in ink, being careful not to make a mistake or any mess in this very important book.

The rewards of travelling to different areas in England was certainly paying dividends, especially when you knew that being restricted to the Leicester area gave the trainspotter no opportunity to see the vast majority of engines that worked elsewhere. It was a fact that a lot of steam locomotives we sought would never venture to, or pass through, our area, so travel was essential.

Like most families back then mine didn't own a motor vehicle, so travel by public transport was our one and only option. Certainly we ventured to the seaside on the East Coast for family holidays, but the idea of travelling to a city like Bristol, or other areas around the country, was unheard of. I soon realised that our hobby presented me with the opportunity of seeing a lot of England in the early 1960s that I wouldn't otherwise have seen, and looking back I think I was very lucky to be able to do so.

For example, on Sunday 17 July 1960 we joined the Great Central Club's shed trip to the Liverpool area, which proved quiet memorable, starting with awful weather that saw us boarding the coach in Leicester soaking wet thanks to continuous pouring rain. The downpour eventually ceased and the Club's drying members trudged around a record number of 11 sheds in the North West. A memory of mine from the day is of our coach being held up not far from the famous Mersey Tunnel by a large procession of Liverpool seamen who were on strike at the time. When I reminded Big Stu about it he said that a certain person was very brave, shouting abuse at them as they were marching in large numbers behind their big red Union Banner; he added that I soon shut up when we pulled up at a set of traffic lights, with the marchers catching up fast. What both of us had completely forgotten about was that on our return journey our coach ran out of fuel at Markfield, just north of Leicester, having consumed 36 gallons. I can only assume that we were not far from a petrol station, because despite the problem we managed to refuel and reach home by 10.30pm.

OK, so how did I know it was pouring with rain, and about the fuel problem? Well, I've been very fortunate because the Great Central Railway Club produced regular newsletters from 1960 detailing short reports of its trips, together with some photographs that have come to light after 50 years, but more about that later. Looking back on my trip records compared to previous shed visits, this one brought home the unglamorous side of our hobby, with shed after shed being filled with dirty and grimy freight engines only, although the old Lancashire & Yorkshire 0-6-0s at Lees (Oldham) and Bury were interesting to come across, together with the small 0-4-0 dock shunters. Even Liverpool's famous Edge Hill shed (8A) was a little disappointing, with no 'Coronation' 'Pacifics' present, although thankfully a couple of the depot's 'Princess Royals' were. I suppose the 'star find' of the day was No 45552 *Silver Jubilee*, the very first of Stanier's 'Jubilee' engines, which had very unusual chrome-plated silver cab numbers, and nameplates.

What I didn't know at the time of our visit to Liverpool during that summer of 1960 was that there was an unknown group of young lads in a local musical band performing in the city, called the 'Silver Beetles', who would eventually become rather famous under a slightly different name. I wonder if any of the lads used to train-spot…

With the Club's trips coming thick and fast, I was gaining more friends thanks to our shared hobby, including Grammar School boys. Yes, they thought they were a lot cleverer than us, a bit snobby, and a little standoffish to start with, but we were soon to make a breakthrough when one of my friends, Mick Combey, started to bring a small stock of Mars bars and Wagon Wheels on the trips from the wholesaler where he worked, and we helped him sell them from the back seat of the coach for what we thought was a small profit, which wasn't quite true when he admitted many years later that they never cost him anything. I'll leave the rest to your imagination! Now, if there's one thing any 13-year-old boy can't resist it's chocolate, especially in the days when motorway service stations were rare, and shops were closed on Sundays, so we had a captive market. I'd like to tell you that

A photograph of No 45552, which I was lucky enough to be given by one of my school pals on the trip, Stan Richardson.

from there Mick went on to build a shopping empire, but sadly he didn't, nor went to prison, but thanks to him we became very popular with all concerned and the social barriers were broken, and Mick? Well, he did become a policeman for a short while.

Another thing about these trips was the attitude of our parents to our adventures. It seems strange in this day and age to say that none of my friends and I enjoyed the luxury of having a telephone at home. Looking back at the shed visiting destinations, we hadn't a clue what time we would arrive back home, so we couldn't ring and advise them. We were also usually dropped off back in town, needing then to catch a late bus home, so it must have been a relief when we arrived, often late, very tired and dirty. I know my parents never showed the slightest interest in trains, especially my Dad, who was football mad, while I wasn't, so not a lot of bonding there. But, bless him, he put up with his son's passion and never actually stopped me enjoying my travels.

I mentioned before that by 1960 I had already seen a large number of British Railways steam locomotives. The most exciting for me were always the named engines, and the numbers I had observed I counted in August of that year with the following results:

Great Western	223
Southern Region	2
Midland Region	309
Great Eastern	122
BR Standards	26
Grand total	682

Looking at these details you may notice that only a couple of Southern namers had been observed, which was a major disappointment and completely out of proportion compared with the other regions, but the opportunity to travel south often had yet to present itself, so understandably hardly any of the region's locomotives had been noted, leaving the Southern section of my Ian Allan *abc* with just a few underlinings compared to other regions, something I was determined to rectify.

To its credit, the Great Central Club was beginning to help, planning in the future to spread its wings far and wide over BR's regions, so hopefully it would only be a matter of time before we would be able to visit Southern territory. Although I didn't appreciated it at the time, I think our Society's organisation must have been first class, with trips organised and shed permits obtained for all the sheds we visited, something we as individuals at our age would have found impossible to get. We certainly preferred the official visit than trying to 'bunk' a shed, with the threat of capture and a stern lecture regarding trespass on BR property from the shed foreman or, worse, the local bobby. So good was the Club's organisation that I can't remember on any of our trips ever struggling to locate an engine shed, which seems amazing to me now, considering the many areas we visited. The navigation must have been spot-on to enable us to find so many of the depots that we managed seamlessly to visit, especially with many of them tucked away in some rough and obscure part of a city or town.

After our Liverpool outing we ventured a lot closer to home

at the end of August with a Sunday visit to the Nottingham and Sheffield area sheds. During this trip I remember being surprised to find trams and trolleybuses still working in both cities. Strangely for me, observing the trams in Sheffield, rather than the trains, proved one of the highlights of the day as, despite a large number of engines recorded, very few of my favourite express locomotives were seen. At least we did get to see some of the famous ex-Great Central Railway 'Director' 4-4-0s Nos

Mexborough GC (41F) Sunday 28 August 1960	
Class	**Number/Name**
2-6-2T Class 3	40190
2-8-0 8F	48088, 48615
2-6-2 'V2'	60897
4-6-0 'B1'	61083, 61165, 61166, 61170, 61374
2-6-0 'K3'	61822, 61908, 61959, 61966, 61981, 61984
0-6-0 'J11'	64377, 64402, 64407, 64417, 64425, 64442
2-8-0 'O1'/'O4'	63588, 63593, 63597, 63612, 63622, 63623, 63628, 63648, 63653, 63659, 63665, 63669, 63681, 63684, 63685, 63702, 63718, 63738, 63772, 63774, 63779, 63798, 63813, 63828, 63829, 63837, 63841, 63853, 63862, 63883, 63884, 63897, 63901, 63904, 63907, 63917
2-8-0 'WD'	90065, 90085, 90118, 90119, 90151, 90203, 90209, 90211, 90220, 90250, 90252, 90330, 90384, 90400, 90421, 90440, 90491, 90521, 90528, 90567, 90590, 90608, 90627
Diesel shunter	D3333

Nottingham (16A)	
2-6-2T Class 4	42185, 42636
0-6-0 4F	43888, 43911, 43928, 43953, 43954, 43958, 44039, 44047, 44151, 44248
4-6-0 Class 5	44759, 44860, 45399
4-6-0 'Jubilee'	45579 *Punjab*
4-6-0 'Royal Scot'	46116 *Irish Guardsman*
0-6-0T 3F	47272, 47631
2-8-0 8F	48211, 48374, 48614, 48653, 48696
0-8-0 7F	48898
4-6-0 BR Class 5	73136
4-6-0 BR Class 4	75062
2-6-0 BR Class 2	78020, 78021

62664 *Princess Mary* and 62668 *Jutland*, despite a number of the class already withdrawn still being in service at Sheffield Darnell.

To be fair, I did gain an insight into the huge railway freight business of the area, particularly the coal industry servicing the Nottinghamshire and Yorkshire coalfields, and the huge amount of locomotives required. One only has to look at Mexborough shed (41F) in the accompanying table to see the large number of 'ROD' 2-8-0s and 'Austerities' observed to see what I mean, and for the record I've added our neighbouring Nottingham Midland shed, without a diesel in sight.

Now let's return to the subject of keeping trip records of engines seen, which I'm sure you will agree I'd made a pretty good job of so far, being only 13, but at this point, sadly, it all goes pear-shaped again, as they disappear for nearly a year until August 1961. The good news, however, is that, thanks to regular reports of its outings being published in the Great Central Club's magazine, I can identify some of our lost spotting destinations during this period, starting on Saturday 25 November 1960. This was a Club visit to the Sheffield-Manchester electrified main line over the Pennines and, following a major investment of my pocket money in a new Kodak Brownie 127, I was keen to make use of my new purchase for the very first time. About 26 members went on this trip, and were split up into small parties and dropped off at various points along the line with a plan to conduct a survey of passing traffic. Unfortunately it turned out to be a cold and miserable day, and eight of us found ourselves at a rather bleak station at Dinting, where we soon became very bored, eventually deciding to break rank and catch a local electric train to the new Manchester Piccadilly station, the former London Road, which had been rebuilt and renamed for the new London Midland Region electric train services that had started a couple of months before. My memories of the day are limited, but I did take a picture at the station of an English Electric Type 4 diesel standing alongside a new E3000-series Bo-Bo Class A electric locomotive. Despite the new electric network, we did manage to see one steam engine, a 2-8-0 'ROD' in one of the yards outside Manchester, shunting. When my film was developed, disappointment all round as it produced some awful very dark pictures thanks to the wet and dull weather we experienced, and certainly not good enough for inclusion here.

Incidentally, switching to modern times I recently came across an old 127 camera at a car boot sale, and took the opportunity to examine it and look through the camera's viewer, which reminded me how limited they were, especially when trying to capture anything moving. I also remember that the camera only allowed you to take eight pictures from the 127 films available, the cost of which, plus developing, certainly limited me to using only one film on most trips. I'm glad to say that despite my disappointment I wasn't put off, and did get to use the 127 successfully, including during a visit to Doncaster Works, where the accompanying picture of 'A4' No 60012 *Commonwealth of Australia* was taken on an unknown date in 1960.

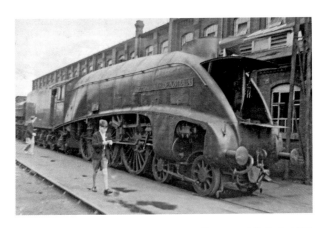

'A4' No 60012 *Commonwealth of Australia* at Doncaster Works in 1960. Please note the short trousers being worn by one of our party.

Also photographed at Doncaster Works that day was a very run-down 'Britannia', No 70054 *Dornoch Firth*, minus its tender. I think she may have been allocated to Leeds Holbeck at this time. I admit it was not the best subject to select with the pile of debris in front of the loco, but it's my photo and it's over 50 years old!

1961

Thanks to the Great Central Club we were all now shed-bashing regulars, with our appetite for collecting numbers fuelled even more by the potential of some of the larger sheds we could visit, especially those in the North West and Carlisle, to where the Club announced it was arranging its first weekend trip in March 1961. This was thrilling news for us young lads, especially after viewing photographs of visiting Scottish Stanier 'Pacifics' at Carlisle, which featured regularly in our *Trains Illustrated* magazines, as did the prospect of seeing some of the rare Standard 'Clan' 'Pacifics' that were stationed at the famous Kingmoor shed, 12A. Naturally all of us lads were desperate to go, and I remember being quite nervous asking my parents, as this would be my very first overnight stay away on my own without them. Thankfully they agreed as long as we all stuck together, and I funded the cost, which came to £3 10s. More good news was confirmed after I contacted the other boys and learned that their parents had also agreed – perhaps another indication of the more relaxed attitude we boys enjoyed growing up in the 1960s.

It was to be a weekend away staying over two nights in a boarding house in Blackpool. What do you think us youngsters were advised by the Society to take with us? Well, their 'Final Trip Details' note read as follows:

'You are reminded that you will need the following items for this trip: toilet requisites (hand-towel, soap, toothbrush, comb, etc), pyjamas, mac, spare socks if required.'

I think that, looking at the list, you may have noticed how things were different in those days, with no mention of underwear or clothes apart from socks to change into, so we off we went on Friday and wore what we stood in until late Sunday! Sandwiches were also available both on the Saturday and Sunday at 2s 6d per day – Big Stu remembers that they were wrapped in newspaper! Sadly again my written records of the locomotives present on the weekend were to disappear; however, I did have my Kodak 127 camera with me, so once again combining some of my photographs taken with a report of the trip that appeared in one of those early Great Central Society magazines, we can retrace our steps all those years ago.

Our adventure started on a dull Friday teatime on 24 March when we boarded the Club's coach at our pick-up point in Woodgate to travel up to Blackpool, where we eventually arrived around 11.00pm at our lodgings, a boarding house just off the seafront. Once there we discovered that all four of us – Big Stu, Stan, Colin and me – would be sharing a room together. Needless to say, as this was our first time away together, very little sleep was achieved, but we did find out about who could pass wind best, and whose socks did require changing!

Mr Appleyard, the boarding house owner, gets a mention in the Club magazine 'as he proved to be a very amiable fellow who had soon christened every member of the party with fictitious names, ranging from "The Beverley Sisters" to just "Dad".' On to the Saturday morning, following an excellent breakfast served by a very nice waitress, we started out for our first shed visit to 24J, Lancaster, which proved very disappointing as few of its allocated engines were present. Then came 24L, Carnforth, and a shock. Upon entering the shed area we found two 'Princess Royals', Nos 46203 and 46211, stored in the yard without nameplates, and their chimneys covered. It was a surprise, and I found it hard to get my head around the fact that their future looked bleak, even for powerful 'Pacific' engines, having not realised the full effect that the introduction of the Type 4 diesels was having on their duties. We then travelled north around Morecambe Bay to Barrow-in-Furness, where my 127 captured 'Jubilee' No 45591 *Udaipur* coupled to 4F No 44443.

Workington, our next stop, was a larger than expected shed, and contained mainly 'Jinties' and 4Fs. We then set out for our main destination of the day, Carlisle. At this point I think it's

4F No 44443 and 'Jubilee' No 45591 *Udaipur* in the shed yard at Barrow-in-Furness.

worth reminding ourselves that these were the days prior to the opening of the M6, and subsequently road transport was a lot slower; to really bring home how different the times were, about 6 miles south of Carlisle our driver, Mr Davis, calmly informed our trip organisers that the coach was almost out of petrol, and sure enough as we climbed a fairly large hill it ground to a halt a few yards from the top. Of course there were no such things as mobiles to ring for help in those days, so Tony Moore and other committee members were soon off the coach and started to flag down passing motorists to establish where the nearest garage was, learning from one of them that it was about a mile and half away; fortunately for us about half of this was downhill. So what do you do in 1961 when your coach runs out of fuel? Well, it's simple – you push it. Thirty-odd of us all jumped off the coach and proceeded first to push it over the brow of the hill then, after it had coasted to a stop at the bottom, pushed it the remaining distance to the 'Esso sign', where, having obtained 20 gallons of petrol, we set off again with a loud cheer.

Before we go any further I should like to add a couple of my own personal memories of our journey that afternoon, starting with us listening on the coach's radio to live commentary of the

Grand National race from Aintree, won by the grey Nicholas Silver, then the passing round among the boys of a certain new book, which had up to recently been banned, *Lady's Chatterley's Lover*, with certain chapters being read out loud at the back of the coach. I, of course, had nothing to do with this disgraceful behaviour, nor could I understand what the older boys were on about anyway.

On reaching Carlisle our first shed visit was 12A, Kingmoor, where the first two locomotives we came across were a 2-10-0 'Austerity', No 90763, and an old Caledonian 0-6-0, No 57653. Our Great Central Club magazine report describes our party then finding a line of 30 engines containing about 16 'Jubilees', including some Scottish ones from Corkerhill shed (67A), also noting two more stored 'Princess Royals', Nos 46201 *Princess Elizabeth* and 46210 *Queen Maud*, and three of the 'Clan' 'Pacifics'.

For us spotters, 'Kingmore' certainly came up to our

No 46226 *Duchess of Norfolk* stands in the shed yard at Carlisle Kingmoor. On the left the lads from our party are making their way between a couple of Class 5 4-6-0s, one of which is fitted with a snowplough.

expectations, especially with the large number of 'Pacifics' on shed, including No 46226 *Duchess of Norfolk*. As mentioned earlier, our visit also provided us with the sight of some of those rare BR 'Clan' 'Pacifics' we were longing to see, brilliant 'cops' for us because of their Scottish and Northern allocation. One I remember was No 72005 *Clan Macgregor* stabled in the shed yard next to 'Britannia' 4-6-2 No 70052 *Firth of Tay*, then shedded at the famous 66A, Glasgow Polmadie shed.

Leaving Kingmoor we then moved on to Carlisle Canal (12C), a really interesting shed, which contained a number of North British engines including No 62484 *Glen Lyon*, one of the surviving five members of the famous 'D34' Class; she was in the company of a number of Eastern Region 'Pacifics' on shed, including Haymarket's 'A4' No 60024 *Kingfisher*. I remember I was very keen to photograph both the 'Glen' and the 'A4' individually, but unfortunately when my 127 film was developed some idiot (me!) had managed to get both engines on the same negative. I was so upset I've kept the negative for 50 years to remind me of the missed opportunity.

Our last Carlisle shed visit was 12B, Upperby, which proved very uninteresting other than its roundhouse building, which was identical to our own Leicester Midland shed (15C). Our day concluded by travelling that evening back via Shap to Blackpool, stopping at a transport café en route.

I'm sure we were pretty exhausted, so we all enjoyed a decent night's sleep at our boarding house before having breakfast, which Big Stu reminded me included laver bread (made from seaweed), a delicacy that Mr Appleyard and his wife insisted we eat before they would allow us to leave the dining room, eventually agreeing to let us out only if we took any leftovers with us wrapped in napkins. So what do you think happened to our hosts as they stood on their doorstep waving us off? Well, suddenly they were bombarded by laver bread thrown through our coach windows. I, of course, never took part in such unsavoury behaviour.

So on to Sunday 26 March, when we started our day by visiting the two Blackpool sheds, North and Central. Our next shed was Fleetwood (24F), and we were given two options to get there – either in our coach, or by a tram ride from Queen's Terrace – so with Big Stu's love of buses, etc, we caught the tram, which dropped us off quite close to the shed's entrance. The depot itself was disappointing, containing only a number of stored locomotives, but the tram was great.

We then travelled on to Preston shed, where I managed to take a decent picture of 'Patriot' Class No 45501 *St Dunstan*. Perhaps the extra light available helped, as the shed roof had been destroyed by a fire in June 1960, and I'm pretty certain it was never rebuilt. Regarding *St Dunstan*, I'd seen her before at Rugby in the shed yard, and seem to remember that she wasn't kept in the normal Brunswick Green livery then, but painted black in tribute to the 'fallen' of the First World War. She was withdrawn a year later.

Lostock Hall (24C) followed, then Lower Darwen shed (24D) at Blackburn, where my Kodak 127 recorded very dirty 'Jubilee' No 45652 *Hawke* (another poor photo), before we

My photograph records the scene at 24E, Blackpool North, with one of the new prototype Derby Sulzer 'Peaks', No D2 *Helvellyn*, standing outside the depot in the company of 8F No 48267 and 'Jubilee' No 45571 *South Africa*.

'Patriot' Class No 45501 *St Dunstan* at Preston shed.

travelled on to Accrington shed, which had recently been closed. Continuing our return journey home that Sunday, we travelled to locomotive sheds on the Settle & Carlisle route, our first port of call being 24H, Hellifield, where we came across Gresley 'A3' No 60038 *Firdaussi*, one of the class newly allocated to Leeds Holbeck (55A), standing in the shed yard.

Skipton shed (24G) was our last port of call that weekend. Here we had a stroke of luck when the 'Thames-Clyde Express' passed through the station hauled by another Holbeck 'A3', No 60077 *The White Knight*. I mentioned earlier about details of our weekend being reported in the Great Central Club's magazine, and copies were passed on to me by Mr Tony Moore himself after I bumped into him quite unexpectedly, having not seen him for – wait for it – 50 years! It was a great surprise and joy to meet up with him again, as I learned that he still had various items of paperwork covering the Club's activities from the early 1960s when I was a member. After revealing to him that I was trying to write a book, he was kind enough to let me have two very old box files that contained items full of information about

Some of our Carlisle weekend party standing outside Hellifield station shortly after our visit to the shed there on Sunday 26 March 1961. Tony's picture was a real surprise, with yours truly aged 14 striking a very strange pose on the left; I have to say that the gabardine mac does me no favours, but it is nice to see that the Kodak 127 camera had a case! Also in the picture is our coach driver, Mr Davis, and in his brown jacket at the front is my old school pal Colin Field. 'Big Stu' and Stan Richardson were, I assume, lagging behind, so missed the photo opportunity, which is a pity, but it was brilliant for me to see this picture after so many years, especially with it being in colour.

our trips, meetings, etc. I couldn't believe my luck, even more so when he provided me with various photographs, including the accompanying one of our party at Hellifield.

Back home, I've already mentioned earlier that we all owned bicycles, which gave us a lot of independence, although the thought of cycling 20-odd miles to either Nuneaton or Rugby and back from Leicester on a heavy bike with few gears might not seem attractive to youngsters nowadays, but we loved it.

On the way to Nuneaton I remember that one of the challenges we set ourselves was not to stop and put our feet down when climbing up the steep hill into Earl Shilton. Believe me, it was a real struggle to keep going, requiring you to stand up on your pedals while in the lowest gear to keep the bike's wheels slowly turning, but when you succeeded and the summit was reached, what a sense of achievement, often celebrated by passing round the Mars bars, as we waited for one of the other boys, who had failed our challenge, having to push his bike up the hill's final few yards to join us. It's amazing looking back now how we never seemed to consider that we could experience a problem on these bike rides like breaking down, or that the weather would turn horrible – we just got on with it, wearing our school uniforms of course, not forgetting shirt and tie. We certainly must have looked smart, this even being acknowledged at a school assembly one morning when our headmaster, Mr Payne, announced that our group of boys, recognised by our school uniforms, had been seen cycling in Warwickshire by an unnamed member of staff. 'A credit to the school,' he said. Obviously we were behaving ourselves, and luckily not slipstreaming at speed down a hill close behind a lorry, the thought of which now does make me think we must have been oblivious to danger, or just plain daft. Our cycling exploits did over the next year or so become even more adventurous, as we spread our wings further and further, with trips to Rugby, Grantham, Derby and even Peterborough and March. I must have been a very fit lad then.

At this point I think we had better get back to Leicester's railways, the Great Central and me saving lives! My story begins with the appearance of the prototype gas turbine locomotive No

I recently discovered a couple of pictures of us taken in 1960 on our beloved bikes, so here's one of Stan, Colin and me in our school uniforms, and all in shirts and ties of course.

GT3, which had been built by English Electric and was tested through Leicester on the Great Central line for six months during 1961. The interesting thing about this engine was that, unlike any diesel, it had a 4-6-0 wheel arrangement just like a steam locomotive, so was truly different and became a sought-after engine to see. I was out and about one weekend with my school chum Mick Harby when we heard through the spotters' grapevine that GT3 was at the Great Central shed, so off we shot to see her.

I mentioned earlier that the shed was situated by the side of the Grand Union Canal in Leicester, and our usual access was from Upperton Road, using the canal path by the road bridge. I remember it was a lovely summer's Sunday afternoon and Mick and I cycled down the gravel path missing the various potholes towards the shed, happily chatting away. Suddenly I heard a splash, and Mick wasn't there any more – he was in the canal with his bike.

Luckily he surfaced quite close to the edge of the canal path, shouting and flapping around in the water. Instinctively I leaned over the water's edge, holding on to some shrubbery, grabbed his arm and managed to hold on to him until a man suddenly appeared and helped me pull him out. Mick was freezing and shaking like a leaf, so we took him to a house nearby to recover. It turned out that it was a lock-keeper's house, where Mick was cared for. I remember him sitting down in front of a stove with towels wrapped around him while I and the lock-keeper went back to fish out his bike, which we eventually managed using some hooks. Motor transport was eventually arranged to take Mick home; he was pretty shaken up, and I promised to get his bike back there for him.

With no transport options to call on, I walked, taking both

Gas turbine locomotive No GT3 – well, part of her! – at Leicester's Great Central shed.

bikes with me, the three or four miles to where he lived. When I arrived I remember being met by his Mum at the front garden gate, who told me that poor Mick was OK, but in bed. She never asked me in, but after taking his bike from me she gave me a half-a-crown (2s 6d in pre-decimalisation money) for my trouble, and thanked me. I'm glad to say Mick survived the ordeal and many years later, when I used to bump into him in a pub in Glenfield, he was kind enough to buy me a pint or two on the basis of me having saved his life, but always mentioned his disgust that his Mum only valued him at half-a-crown! As for No GT3, I did eventually get to see and photograph her at 15E, the GC shed, before she disappeared into railway history.

Much to my father's disappointment I wasn't interested in football, even when Leicester City reached the FA Cup Final in early May 1961. Far more interesting for me were the number of 'Royal Scots' and rebuilt 'Patriots' that appeared at the Great Central shed in preparation for hauling the city's football specials to London. At least three 'Royal Scots' and two 'Patriots' arrived and caused great excitement, as for us they were among the first Midland express locomotives to be seen at the shed. I remember that the boys and I visited the depot on the Friday evening prior the Final to find the express 4-6-0 locomotives looking in wonderful condition, with even their buffers burnished and shinning – what a sight! It didn't take much imagination, with the 'Scots' including Nos 46140 and 46160 and 'Patriot' No 45532 standing there in the yard, for us to pretend that Leicester Central shed was for a few hours a top-link motive power depot, and the local railway staff certainly did a wonderful job turning out the locomotives as they did. That is not to forget Leicester's own 'V2', No 60890, which was also suitably cleaned and joined the distinguished visitors the following morning taking the City fans to London. And the match? Well, Tottenham Hotspur beat the 'Foxes' 2-0, and Dad, who had watched it on our 14-inch black and white TV, was grumpy for a day or two after, bemoaning City's luck.

Staying with the GC, the effects of the decision a few years

Many years after Cup Final day, I was thrilled to find Colin Walker's photograph showing the Great Central shed yard that evening, included in his wonderful book *Great Central Twilight*. Colin Walker

earlier to transfer the control of the line to the London Midland Region was by now becoming clear even to us youngsters. The run down of its services had already begun, sadly with the loss of the line's prestigious named expresses, the 'Master Cutler' and the 'South Yorkshireman', then the introduction of a semi-fast service between Nottingham and Marylebone. It did, however, retain trains of interest for us spotters, particularly the Bournemouth to York service, which often brought a Great Western 'Hall' to the Central station; the engine usually returned to Banbury on an early evening local to Woodford Halse. There was also the Grimsby to the West of England fish train, which as you will discover later was to become a firm favourite with us local enthusiasts in the coming years.

Despite the loss of my own spotting observations, and thanks once again to the records I received from Tony, I know that our next GC Club trip took place on Sunday 30 April 1961, when we visited the Bristol area and, for the first time, Swindon's railway works and shed. This was followed a month later on 28 May when we joined what was advertised as a 'Southern Region

Colin Walker's book also contains a picture of an Ian Allan enthusiasts' special from Marylebone to Doncaster Works passing through our city hauled by none other than the famous No 60103 *Flying Scotsman*. It was taken the year before, in April 1960, and not only did I see her, but I was actually standing there below on the Abbey Pastures, on the left-hand side of the picture, watching her pass by. I thought the picture was worth including as it helped bring back an event that I'd actually forgotten about until reading his book. *Colin Walker*

Outing', which went to the London area. It was reported thus:

'At 6.15am on Sunday 28th May a coach-load of GCRS members left Leicester by the Aylestone Road en route for the M1 and Watford, the first shed. This produced mainly its own allocation, but an English Electric Type 4 D340 passed by on a Perth-London Sleeping Car Express.

Next shed on the itinerary was Southall, which contained a wide range of classes from 57XX pannier tanks to 47XX 2-8-0s and 9Fs. Most interesting locos found were 8422 (83D), and a Hall 6909 (88A). Some members were disappointed at not seeing any ex-Great Western railcars, as these had recently been moved into store at Kidderminster.

We then moved on to the Southern sheds, starting with Feltham on which were 13 Q1s and a "King Arthur", *Sir Hedimere*; also noted was a "Schools" Class 4-4-0, *Christ's Hospital*.

Guildford was next, where all three of its "Schools" were observed along with one of the remaining B4 0-4-0s, 30089, the shed pilot. An Exmouth Junction N Class, No 31834, was observed along with many of Guildford's own allocation of this engine type.

Redhill Shed produced no surprises with a D1 and CZX stored, then a short run passing Gatwick Airport brought us to Three Bridges, which contained many of its Ks, and a Brush diesel D5613 was noted passing by on a South Coast Excursion.

Another short run then took us to Tonbridge; where some of its H tanks were observed including 31512, sometime star of ITV's "The Old Push and Pull". The shed also contained one of the last three E1 4-4-0s, and presented most members with their first sight of D6500s.

Hither Green which followed was flooded with these objects; however, there was some steam interest with all but one of the depot's W 2-6-4Ts present, which worked cross-London freights.

Bricklayers Arms, which is due to close later this year, contained one of the other two E1s, 31507. In the works were 34018, 34027 and two diesels D2278, D5017.

Nine Elms still contained many stored 4-4-0s (Classes L, LI, X, D1), Standard Class 5 namers 73082, 73083, and 73118, plus five Schools were also present.

Stewarts Lane, the last shed visited, produced electrics 20001 and 20002 built at Ashford in 1941 as well as several Doncaster-built ones. More "Schools" Class locomotives were noted, some minus their nameplates. The most interesting engines there were the L. B. Billinton-designed E2 Tanks.'

Although no record survives of engine numbers observed on this trip, I do have some photographs I took on that day, including two taken at 70A, Nine Elms shed, of 'Battle of Britain' No 34062 *17 Squadron*. The first was of its large nameplate, which

'Battle of Britain' No 34062 *17 Squadron* at Nine Elms.

was of a style I had not seen before and must have impressed me; the second, included here, shows the 'Pacific' and the tell-tale blocks of towering flats in the background, which help to identify this famous shed. I don't know what they were thinking about in those days building new housing blocks next door to one of London's very busy, smoky and large dirty engine sheds. I'm sure the local corner laundry driers must have done a roaring trade, as it certainly was not the place to hang out the clean laundry to dry!

Having mentioned that the trip report appeared in the GC Club's 1961 Summer Review, the magazine not only featured another outing to Crewe and Chester, to which I refer below, but also an article by yours truly about the 'A4' 'Pacifics', which was to be one of a number of similar articles I was to come across in later editions, none of which surprisingly I can remember writing, but there they are, another interesting find for me from more than 50 years ago.

So on to Sunday 16 July 1961, and our Club's trip to Crewe, Chester and Shrewsbury, details of which were reported in the Review by a friend, John Worley.

'On this rather wet morning forty members of the GCRS left

Leicester with the aim of visiting fifteen sheds in the Crewe area. After driving through the bleak Potteries we arrived at our first shed, Stoke, clad in our mackintoshes. This produced mainly Jinties and 4F 0-6-0s besides a large number of Crabs, one of which belonged to Longsight shed.

We then proceeded via Alsager (more 0-6-0s) to Crewe, where members wanting to see "namers" were not disappointed. Crewe North yielded about twenty including the double-chimney "Jubilee" 45556 *Bahamas*, and the surviving rebuilt "Claughton" 45501 *St Dunstan*.

Next we visited Gresty Lane, which contained "Hall" 4-6-0s, and then Crewe South where amongst engines awaiting the works we found 41268 ex-Leicester 15C, also "Princess Royal" 46212, which will most likely be scrapped. We then continued

No 46251 *City of Nottingham* at Crewe North shed on 16 July.

our journey to 6A Chester Midland shed where we encountered two "Castle" class 4-6-0s, 5033 and 7026. Also noted was 5399 from Croes Newydd.

Following there our journey took us across the Welsh border to Mold Junction where we observed amongst other Western engines 2855 of 89B. Croes Newydd was our next stop with a number of 22XX 0-6-0s present and 2-6-0 7300. Our journey continued via Ruabon to Oswestry where we visited both shed and works. In the former we saw several Ivatt 2 2-6-0s and a GW "Manor", and a number of diminutive 14XX 0-4-2 tanks. Everyone was pleased to see "Dukedog" 9017, which is to be preserved privately, and 822 and 823 of the Welshpool & Llanfair Light Railway in the works.

We then proceeded to Shrewsbury where on a very busy shed we saw 45726 *Vindictive*, and "Castle" Class 7015 *Carn Brea Castle*. After about three-quarters of an hour we were on our way to Wellington, where we sadly noticed 41900 in a very poor condition.

Moving on towards the West Midlands we first visited Bushbury, which contained an assortment of locos including Type 4 D314, then climbed the hill to Oxley where 3210 of Templecombe was noted after a works visit. Ten minutes after leaving there saw us at 84A Stafford Road, where we saw several "Kings" and "Castles". Our final shed was 21B Bescot, which had a certain ancient air about it with thirty LNW 0-8-0s, several old Midland Class 2 0-6-0s, and two LMS 4-4-0s in steam.'

Now let's return to my own records, which from August 1961

John Worley also kindly gave me his photograph taken that day of 2ft 6in-gauge 0-6-0T No 823 in Oswestry Works.

I'm delighted to say are intact, and also included my engine 'cops' locally at both Leicester Midland and the Great Central during my school summer holidays. Incidentally, I should advise that these recorded observations never covered all locomotives present on shed or those seen passing through, but only those that I had not observed before ('copped') together with some of the most interesting visitors.

These trainspotting records from early August included a fantastic 'cop' for us locals, thanks to the visit of Scottish 'Jubilee' No 45707 *Valiant* of Corkerhill shed (67A), which I assume had arrived on the Carlisle freight and stayed around for a couple of days before returning north. Nuneaton shed (2B) had been allocated a number of the 4-6-0 'Patriot' engines at the beginning of the year, one of which, No 45542, I also recorded. I remember

Leicester Midland, Thursday 3 August 1961	
Class	**Number/Name**
2-6-0 5MT	42762 (12A Carlisle Kingmoor)
4-6-0 'Jubilee'	45707 *Valiant* (67A Corkerhill Glasgow)
2-8-0 8F	48137, 48374, 48443 (55A Leeds Holbeck)
4-6-0 Class 5	44757, 45078
2-10-0 BR 9F	92159
Leicester Great Central	
4-6-2 'A3'	60110 *Robert the Devil*
4-6-0 'B1'	61249 *Fitzherbert Wright*, 61381, 61178
2-8-0 'WD'	90695 (50A York)
2-10-0 BR 9F	92078, 92068
Leicester Midland, Sunday 5 August 1961	
2-6-0 5MT	42832 (Carlisle Kingmoor)
0-6-0 4F	44038 (24E Blackpool)
4-6-0 'Jubilee'	45707 *Valiant* (67A Corkerhill Glasgow)

4-6-0 Class 5	45006, 45260 (both 17A Derby)
4-6-0 'Patriot'	45542 (2B Nuneaton)
4-6-0 'Royal Scot'	46143 *The South Staffordshire Regiment*
2-8-0 'WD'	90305 (31B March)
Leicester Great Central	
2-6-2 'V2'	60967 (34E Grantham), 60975 (50A York)
4-6-0 'B1'	61011 *Waterbuck*
EE 4-6-0 gas turbine	GT3

they usually turned up on a pick-up freight, which arrived around lunchtime on a Saturday, and were serviced at the shed, turned on the outside turntable and returned back home on a similar train in the afternoon. When researching for my story I was fortunate to come across the accompanying photograph of sister engine No 45537 *Private E. Sykes* V.C., another regular on the freight. It's a particularly evocative picture for me of an unrebuilt 'Patriot' Class engine very smartly turned out by her home depot, because it also features the terraced houses that surrounded the shed area, with the corner of Hutchinson Street rising above the 4F 0-6-0 stabled behind No 45537, and the rear of the Upper Kent Street homes also plainly seen. All were to disappear in one of the city's clearance schemes in the 1970s, together with the small grocery shop where certain friends of mine were always taking empty pop bottles back for refunds, obtaining sweets and Jubblys in return. I was later to discover that they had discovered the shop's back yard where crates of empty bottles were stored, and were helping themselves before returning them as if they had been purchased. I, of course, again had nothing to do whatsoever with such behaviour. Honest!

Turning to the Great Central, although once common it was now very unusual to see a Gresley 'A3' on the line, so *Robert the Devil's* appearance was a pleasant surprise. Sadly I can't remember

'Patriot' No 45537 *Private E. Sykes VC* being turned on the turntable at Leicester Midland shed. *Alec Swain/ transporttreasury.co.uk*

the circumstances of its visit. It was also nice to see a couple of the 'V2s' still around on 15E on the Sunday, although both were visitors, and of course GT3.

A week later I was off to the Norfolk Broads on a school camping holiday, staying in fields at Martham Ferry close to Potter Heigham. I can't remember why I was attracted to go on this holiday, because even my close pals decided not to join me, so I found myself alone very bravely sharing a tent, having never been in one before, with seven other boys from different Leicester schools. Time has robbed me of their names, but the Kodak 127 was there again, so you can see them and our luxurious tent, in which we found ourselves under water following a deluge during the first evening. It was so bad that other boys were transferred the following evening to a local church where they slept on the pews, but we were not so lucky and endured another wet, miserable night until the weather relented.

For me, this holiday soon turned into an even bigger mistake, because it was designed around us boys enjoying the delights of sailing on the Norfolk Broads, and it might not come as much of a surprise to you to learn that I didn't take to it. Nor to a sports day organised by the teachers during the week, when we were

Our luxurious tent on the Norfolk Broads!

made to take part in swimming races in the murky waters close by. Luckily I soon discovered a couple of other boys interested in railways, and on learning that there was a local bus service available close by we soon arranged our alternative agenda, which involved going off trainspotting to Norwich and other places. I even managed to avoid not only the sailing, but also the camp's daily work rota that was sprung on us, in which you were selected in turn to dig trenches for the loos, and work in the camp's kitchens washing up after breakfast and our evening meal. I think they had picked boys by going through surnames in alphabetic order, so my 'W' had saved me. I remember that our absence was noticed by one master, who, when addressing the camp at the end of the week, spoke out about 'certain boys' avoiding the activities that the staff had organised, and not entering into the spirit of the holiday, but I felt no guilt whatsoever and kept a low profile until returning home to dear old Leicester. You see, thanks to trainspotting our little band did enjoy ourselves, but this type of holiday was certainly not for me, and I remember how pleased I felt to return home and see my Mum, whom I'd missed so much, and of course a proper roof over my head.

Obviously by now, thanks to my hobby, I had covered quite a few areas of the country, so it came as a shock to see how much diesels had replaced steam power in the Norwich area. Still, on Tuesday 14 August I did manage to observe the very last 'B12', 4-6-0 No 61572, in service shunting carriage stock at Norwich Thorpe station just a month before she was withdrawn. Later, having decided to take a chance and 'bunk' Norwich shed (go round without permission), we made our way from the station to the entrance of 32A, where we enjoyed a stroke of luck by bumping into another group of lads in a party about to visit. They had an official pass and, after taking pity on us, invited us to join them. Despite the midweek visit, the shed foreman proved really helpful, and provided us with a guide, an old railwayman, to show us round the depot. Following him around, we soon entered a shed where servicing was carried out, and found 'Britannia' No 70035 *Rudyard Kipling* standing cold having just received maintenance, and we were invited by our guide to climb up onto her footplate,

Norwich Thorpe (32A), Tuesday 14 August 1961	
Class	**Number/Name**
Diesel shunters	11111, 11168, D2034, D2037, D2203, D2214
BR Type 2	D5042
Brush Type 2	D5500, D5531, D5535, D5536, D5538, D5555, D5556, D5560, D5561, D5566, D5574, D5575, D5584, D5585, D5589
EE Type 3	D6702, D6720, D6721
EE Type 4	D203, D206
BTH Type 1	D8224
0-6-0 'J19'	64663 (stored withdrawn)
2-6-4T 'L1'	67720, 67723, 67734
4-6-2 'Britannia'	70010 Owen Glendower, 70035 Rudyard Kipling

where he explained the various controls, etc. He then opened the firebox door, revealing the inside of the firebox, which looked vast because it was completely empty. Much to our surprise he then asked for volunteers to climb through the small door into it, an invitation I and a couple of other lads accepted. Having squeezed my way in I remember being able to stand upright on the floor stays, looking at the wall of boiler tubes inside and wondering if I could ever extract myself again. Obviously I did, and only wish that I could be as slim these days. Certainly mission impossible now!

Around this time our attitude to trainspotting

did begin to change, especially in the pursuit of 'namers' and trying to see as many of a particular class of express engines before they were withdrawn. Bearing in mind that by now most of our targets were based outside our local area, research came into the equation, identifying engines we wanted to see with visits planned to the locos' home sheds presenting the best opportunity. Tracking down one of those elusive engines developed into an exciting part of our hobby, especially when you least expected it, gaining a real sense of achievement in doing so.

I think around this time other attitudes started to change with us boys. After all, we were rushing towards the age of 15 in 1961 and, starting our last year at school after the summer break, we were suddenly becoming 'grown-up'. Now, I don't know about you, but confusion reigned within me, especially after I had my first love affair other than with trains. It started when Big Stu, Stan, and I went to the local cinema to see a black and white film that had just been released called *Whistle down the Wind*. In it was a lovely young girl named Hayley Mills, who came across some fellow played by Alan Bates in a barn, and thought he was Jesus. A bit serious I know, except for Miss Mills, who suddenly, unknown to her, had found a new admirer from Leicester. My emotions were further sent into orbit when I saw her in a later film in colour. I thought she was lovely, and did a lot of dreaming about her while trainspotting by the lineside over the next few months. What was happening to me?

I've already mentioned earlier the Derby Works Open Day, which was held every year, and 1961 was no exception. It was organised in August so, without spanners, we decided to visit, catching the train from Leicester. After making the short walk from the Midland station, we joined the queue of excited trainspotters awaiting entry to the works in Siddals Road.

To help give you a flavour of what was happening back then in the works I came across the following diary notes covering that summer's activities:

'In June the Type 4 construction had reached the end of the order, with frames laid up to D49. The quantity and variety of diesels under repair remained at a high level, whilst the repair of steam locomotives continued at a steady rate.

A milestone of sorts was reached on June 20th when D34 was outshopped from the works and reported as the 1,000th main-line diesel locomotive delivered under the Modernisation Plan of 1955. With Derby's existing Type 4 order "completed", new frames were laid for a further order of fifty-six Type 4s starting with D138 and to be equipped with Brush electrical equipment rather than that of Crompton Parkinson. By the time of the July works holiday the frames had been laid up to D141.

Locomotives under repair included three named English Electric Type 4s: D214, D230 and D232. Although some of this Class were named at special ceremonies many received their nameplates while in the works; since Derby made the nameplates it must be assumed that they were also fitted here. Also present for repair was 10203. During August the Type 4 frames were laid up to D143, and the works was the usual mix of steam and diesel repairs.

The Annual Works Open Day during August included maroon-liveried 46254 *City of Stoke-on-Trent*, 92220 *Evening Star* and a brand new Type 4 [later Class 45] in the viewing area.'

My Derby records reflected a busy works with a large production line of new 'Peak' main-line diesels being built, coupled with steam and diesel locomotive repairs. A number of withdrawn engines were also noted, including the odd diesel shunter, and I seem to remember the scrapping of some of the engines locally at the private yard of Albert Looms just down the line at Spondon, which we passed on the way into Derby on our train.

A lot of interest at the Open Day was generated by a large number of Stanier tanks (42500 number series) that had recently been made redundant on the London to Tilbury line, so had spent their working lives not in our area but on the Eastern Region, working out of Fenchurch Street station. Despite many of the engines never returning to traffic, they were for us great 'cops' – as I mentioned before, the chase was on to see as many steam locos as possible, and record them in our *abc* 'Combines'. The works also contained the last 2F tank, No 58850, built in

1879 and withdrawn from Rowsley shed (17D); unknown to us at the time, it was heading for preservation. There was also one of the few surviving Midland 'Compounds', No 41168, and one of Leicester's old 2P 4-4-0s, No 40402; a really interesting visitor was one of the Somerset & Dorset 2-8-0s, No 53809.

Having been around the works, we also ventured into Derby to Friargate, where the Great Northern line could be seen, and where we added a couple of Eastern engine numbers – 'B1' No 61093 and 'K3' No 61959 – to the day's collection, before catching a 'Peak'-hauled express back home to Leicester.

In September a second weekend away was organised by the Great Central Society, on the 16th and 17th, this time to Wales, covering lots of sheds I'd never visited before, with the prospect of lots of steam on offer. This was a trip that attracted my old school friends as well, despite the fact that they were no longer my classmates, since I was now on my own, having been judged capable of taking GCEs. Unfortunately the educational culture shock eventfully proved too much for me, but more about that later.

This turned out to be an eventful weekend, during which things did not go to plan when our coach arrived at Carmarthen on the Saturday evening requiring repairs. We had travelled down to Rhyl in North Wales the previous Friday evening, and on the Saturday morning, with a full day of shed visits ahead, we started after breakfast at the local shed, Rhyl (6K). We then moved down the coast to Llandudno and Bangor, then on to Barmouth around lunchtime, where we stopped for fish and chips from a local chippy just across from the station. It's strange what you remember – at Barmouth it was the wind blowing sand into my chips! During the rest of the day we visited Machynlleth, Aberystwyth and Goodwick before arriving at Carmarthen that evening with a distinct smell of burning, and the coach in trouble – its offside rear wheels were binding.

I remember – we all remember – the nice welcome we received at Mrs Reaves's boarding house, where we were to stay the night. You see, she had a couple of lovely daughters – I told you our attitudes were changing – and our coach problems were soon forgotten.

The following morning we made the perfect start to the day,

Locomotives on display at Derby Works Open Day in 1961. *Tony Moore*

when one of her daughters served us our bacon and eggs, making a lovely fuss of us and bending over the breakfast table with a number of her blouse buttons undone, revealing … well, I'll leave the rest to your imagination. When she returned to the kitchen we heard raised voices speaking Welsh as Mrs Reaves must have noticed her daughter's attire, and she returned with the toast with her buttons done up to her neck, and looking rather sheepish. Needless to say, 50 years ago that young lady certainly made an impression on us lads – it was a lovely way to have breakfast served!

Our group came together later to be informed that the coach was being repaired at a local garage, and would not be available until at least mid-afternoon, so we were free to spend the time how we wished. Someone suggested we should catch a train to Swansea and try to get round a steam shed. This led to a mad dash to the station where, despite the limited Sunday train service, a local for Swansea was standing in the platform waiting to depart as we arrived. Stan and I quickly jumped on with some other boys just as the train pulled out, not realising that Big Stu and Mick Harby had been left behind.

It was a lovely sunny morning, and I remember our three or four carriages were hauled by a 'Castle', No 5027 *Farleigh Castle*, which showed a great turn of speed on our journey to Swansea. Thanks to our Ian Allan Shed Directory we soon found our way to 87D, Swansea East Dock, and easily wandered around the depot feeling a little bit of one-upmanship over our pals who had missed the train. Time was then spent at the station, before we caught our train back, also pulled by a 'Castle', No 5004 *Llanstephan Castle*, and we enjoyed another fine run, returning to brag about our exploits to the rest of the boys as we boarded our repaired coach at just before 5.00pm.

Unfortunately for us, our first port of call after leaving Carmarthen was Swansea East Dock! Everyone proceeded to visit, including Big Stu and Mick, who thought we had wasted a lot of our energy and money (train fare) for nothing – they knew we were visiting the shed so they didn't bother to catch the train. At this point Stan and I hated them, but they had some

My Kodak 127 didn't accompany me on the Welsh weekend, but Stan had his camera, and was kind enough to give me this photo he took of yours truly on the footplate of tank locomotive No 3797 at Swansea East Dock.

sandwiches made up by Mrs Reaves, which they shared with us, as we were starving, so peace was soon declared.

As already mentioned, this weekend wasn't without incident. When we reached Swansea we had arranged to pick up several of the older lads who like us had gone off during the day. Unfortunately they failed to return to the station as arranged, and because we were running late due to the coach repair we had no option but to leave without them, and they were never seen again! What different times these were – there were no mobile phones available to help us keep in touch, nor had we phones at home, so we were unable to contact our parents to let them know we would be late – as it turned out, very, very, late. In fact, it was around 3.00am when we eventually got back to Leicester, and home, where a very worried and upset Mum and Dad were waiting for me. They soon let me know their thoughts on my hobby and me, threatening to cut short my trainspotting days. I remember going to school later that morning and keeping a very low profile for a week or so afterwards.

Finally, before I move on from our weekend trip, I think

it's worth comparing the very different railway scene found in Wales with what I had found on my holiday in Norfolk just over a month before; it was a complete reversal of the diesel situation compared to the Eastern Region. Diesels had no foothold at all in the Welsh areas we visited, with only two main-line engines noted, together with a small number of shunters. Some of the sheds were still 100% steam, a complete turnaround compared

Here's a closer look at the coach used by the Club for all those adventures in the early 1960s, Lester Bros' Bedford SB1 Europa. *Tony Moore*

with the Norwich area, thank goodness.

By the middle of October all was better on the home front, so I was able to join the lads on our second Great Central Railway Society trip to the Liverpool area, with the added interest of visiting sheds we had not covered before in 1961, including Bank Hall, Walton and Aintree. My record book indicates that we managed to visit 12 depots during the Sunday, which was some going, noting 520 locomotives, more than 200 of which I hadn't seen before, despite our previous visit. I was also the writer of a trip report that featured in the Club's Winter Review giving details of our shed visits, so from that I know it was a very foggy morning when our party of 40 set out, and the day out cost 19 shillings.

It was great once more to see a couple of 'Princess Royals'

Liverpool Edge Hill (8A), 15 October 1961	
Class	**Number/Name**
2-6-2T Class 2	41213
2-6-4T Class 4	42153, 42595
2-6-0 5MT	42952
0-6-0 4F	44409
4-6-0 Class 5	44906, 44907, 45034, 45039, 45107, 45242, 45254 45376, 45412, 45421
4-6-0 'Patriot'	45513, 45520 Llandudno, 45524 Blackpool, 45543 Home Guard, 45547
4-6-0 'Jubilee'	45593 Kolhapur, 45603 Solomon Islands, 45671 Prince Rupert
4-6-2 'Princess Royal'	46204 Princess Louise, 46208 Princess Helena Victoria
4-6-2 'Princess Coronation'	46233 Duchess of Sutherland, 46239 City of Chester, 46241 City of Edinburgh, 46243 City of Lancaster
0-6-0T 2F	47166

Liverpool Edge Hill (8A) Continued

0-6-0T 3F	47289, 47353, 47357, 47416, 47453, 47487, 47488, 47512, 47566, 47591, 47617, 47656
2-8-0 8F	48157, 48249, 48259, 48512, 48535, 48742
0-8-0 7F	48926, 49037, 49130, 49137, 49142, 49147, 49155, 49352, 49392, 49394, 49399, 49405, 49412, 49415, 49416, 49432, 49434, 49437
2-8-0 'WD'	90707
Diesel shunters	D2198, D2234, D2373
EE Type 4	D223 Lancastria, D226, D235, D332

Liverpool Bank Hall (27A)

2-6-2T Class 2	41205, 41206, 41268, 41269
2-6-4T Class 4	42120, 42180, 42555
2-6-0 5MT	42856
0-6-0 4F	44462
4-6-0 Class 5	44692, 44743, 44745, 44767, 44895
4-6-0 'Patriot'	45517
4-6-0 'Jubilee'	45717 Dauntless
0-4-0ST 0F	47001, 47002
0-6-0T 3F	47230, 47480, 47550, 47593
0-4-0ST 0F	51206, 51232, 51253
4-6-0 BR Class 4	75045, 75048, 75049
2-6-0 BR Class 2	78040, 78042, 78044, 78060
2-8-0 'WD'	90576
Diesel shunters	D2850, D2852, D2853, D2855, D2857

on Edge Hill shed during the trip. Sadly, unknown to us, one of them, No 46204 *Princess Louise*, had been withdrawn from service earlier that month, and faced the scrapheap together with three of her sisters, Nos 46210/11/12. At a stroke a third of the class had been condemned, leaving most of the other members stored following the end of the 1961 summer service. I always considered them as very powerful express engines, and had many memories of them storming non-stop through Nuneaton and Rugby. At least by then I had managed to observe every member of the famous class in service.

Bank Hall shed (27A) was on Stanley Road close to the dock area, and was accessed through a door in a wall from which we descended a stairway, passing the foreman's office, into the shed. I was really excited to go around there because it was one of those depots whose allocation of engines was rarely seen by Leicester enthusiasts, and it was certainly not a place to take a chance getting around without an official permit.

Towards the end of the day we reached Warrington shed (8B), where we came across a couple of locomotives, 'Jubilee' No 45630 *Swaziland* and Class 5 No 45401, that had been involved in a freight train collision earlier that month. Having sustained damage, they both suffered a similar fate, being withdrawn in early December, with the 'Black 5' being one of the first of its type to be scrapped, yet another sign of the times.

Our cosy steam world was indeed shattering, and our heroes – the express engines – were beginning to disappear, and not just Midland ones – the Eastern Region was starting to condemn its Gresley 'A3' 'Pacifics'. Back home the news on the steam front was a little rosier, when Eastern Region 'Britannias' suddenly appeared regularly at Leicester Midland shed. Our spotters' grapevine soon reported that a number of them had been transferred to March shed (31B), which often provided motive power for the Peterborough passenger service and fitted freights through our area. Encouraged by this development, coupled with our curiosity to see some of the new English Electric Type 5 diesel-electric locomotives, the 'Deltics', in service, a trip to Peterborough soon became a priority for us. Yes, I know it might surprise you that I used the dirty word 'diesel' with such enthusiasm, but according to those that had seen them the 'Deltics' made as much smoke (exhaust) as steam engines, and sounded very powerful, thanks to the noise of their two Napier engines, especially when departing from stations. So would this new diesel get the spotters' hearts racing a little? We were soon to find out with a visit to the East Coast Main Line in late October 1961.

Our eagerly awaited first ever sighting of a 'Deltic' locomotive came soon after arriving at Peterborough, when No D9005 passed through. Watching her accelerate her express train away from the station, I remember thinking that she certainly sounded powerful, and began to understand why it was felt that this type of diesel locomotive appeared different from the rest to such an extent that steam lovers were getting excited about them. Looking at the train service to March, we decided to go there in the early afternoon, allowing us some time during the morning to try our luck at visiting Peterborough's large New England shed (34E), where, despite the absence of an official pass, I'm pleased to say we were successful in sneaking around without being challenged.

Returning to the North station, we joined a large number of

Our first sight of a 'Deltic' was in August 1961. *Tony Moore*

Peterborough New England (34E), 28 October 1961	
Class	**Number/Name**
2-6-0 Class 4	43067, 43082, 43084
4-6-2 'A1'	60143 *Sir Walter Scott*
4-6-2 'A2'	60500 *Edward Thompson*, 60514 *Chamossaire*
2-6-2 'V2'	60820, 60880, 60889, 60912, 60956
4-6-0 'B1'	61070, 61073, 61091, 61174, 61272, 61302, 61332
2-6-0 'K3'	61810, 61830
2-6-0 'K1'	62015
2-6-4T 'L1'	67778, 67792, 67795, 67796, 67798
0-6-0T 'J50'	68896, 68961, 68971, 68976, 68989
0-6-2T 'N2'	69520, 69529, 69575
2-8-0 'WD'	90015, 90055, 90073, 90096, 90146, 90148, 90456, 90473, 90613, 90615, 90618, 90660, 90682
2-10-0 BR 9F	92038, 92039, 92144, 92145, 92183, 92184, 92186, 92196, 92198
Diesel shunters	15004, D3030

enthusiasts gathered at the platform end and recorded a busy period in which three more 'Deltics' appeared, together with a similar number of 'A4s' passing through. I always enjoyed trainspotting at Peterborough, so it brings back some great memories, like the sight and sound of the wheel-tapper busy making his way along a line of carriages on a King's Cross-bound express standing in the platform, the noise of his hammer indicating his progress along the train. Likewise the excitement we felt on hearing the sound of a chime whistle from an approaching 'A4' on a non-stop express, and passing under the majestic bowstring Crescent Bridge that

Peterborough North station

Class	Number/Name
EE Type 5 'Deltic'	D9011
4-6-2 'A4'	60007 Sir Nigel Gresley
4-6-2 'A4'	60008 Dwight D. Eisenhower
2-10-0 BR 9F	92143
4-6-2 'Britannia'	70036 Boadicea
4-6-2 'A4'	60017 Silver Fox
2-8-0 'WD'	90208
4-6-0 Class 5	44660
4-6-2 'A4'	60014 Silver Link
2-8-0 'WD'	90349
4-6-2 'A3'	60061 Pretty Polly
4-6-2 'A1'	60125 Scottish Union
4-6-2 'A1'	60142 Edward Fletcher
2-10-0 BR 9F	92179, 92188
0-6-2T 'N2'	69512, 69579
4-6-2 'A1'	60136 Alcazar
EE Type 5	D9000
2-6-2 'V2'	60869
EE Type 5	D9001
2-6-2 'V2'	60814, 60868
4-6-0 'B1'	61179, 61353
EE Type 4	D286, D273
EE Type 5	D9007
4-6-0 'B1'	61097

dominated the view from the south end of the platforms. Yes, it was a great place to enjoy our hobby, as it seemed to produce an ever-changing procession of trains, from the crack East Coast expresses to summer seaside specials, as well as numerous freight trains, many of which were bound for the large marshalling yards at March. The accompanying table shows the diesel- and steam-hauled main-line express engines, as well as freight, that we witnessed when we returned to the North station from New England shed.

In the early afternoon we caught the local train for a trip down the old Great Eastern line to March, where we were later to be rewarded by seeing five of the newly allocated 'Britannia' 'Pacifics' on shed, one of which, No 70002 *Geoffrey Chaucer*, was a 'cop' for me, as of course were the new 'Deltic' locomotives seen at Peterborough.

Having mentioned the Crescent Bridge at Peterborough, I think it's appropriate we now return to Leicester and have a look at a railway bridge there, which played an important part in our trainspotting. I'm referring to the Swain Street road bridge, which spans the north end of London Road station, and back in the '60s we spotters would climb all over it to get a view of the platforms below. How we enjoyed clambering along the bridge's narrow steelwork girders, despite them being high and narrow, and close above a main city trunk road. Any thoughts of health & safety were certainly not an issue with us, only getting steam 'cops', one of which appeared one Saturday afternoon while I was perched up there looking down on Platform 2, where Bank Hall's 'Jubilee' No 45698 *Mars* arrived.

Interestingly, for many years after the end of steam it was still possible, if you looked closely enough, to make out the numbers of engines long since gone scratched into the bridge's steelwork, often with the dates they were seen – this was all part of the spotters' culture of getting one over on those unfortunates who missed a rare locomotive.

At the end of November 1961 I had just celebrated my 15th birthday, and was having a rough time at school, being unable to step up to the then GCE exam standard with my work. I couldn't

Swain Street bridge spanned the north end of Leicester Midland station. I can't help but think that those short railings were positioned to encourage us spotters to climb up and get a view – they certainly helped, and often you would find four or five of us perched on top on a summer Saturday afternoon. *Leicester Mercury*

cope with the study catch-up workload, and had been switched back to a College of Preceptors class level for my exams the following June. This meant that, instead of staying on for another year, I was going to leave school in August 1962, and finding a job and going to work was now on the horizon. I was growing up, and one of the things reflecting this was my changing circle of friends, not just from school now but also, because of the railway club, more widely spread from all over the city.

I was still in close touch with my old school pals, but I'd become more independent from them. I suppose we were all beginning to do our own thing, which was natural, and by now Mick Harby had certainly packed in trainspotting, which was a pity, especially after I'd saved his life! There was a large group of new lads with whom I was now friendly, including John Elliott, who worked in an administrative position on the railways at the

To prove it, here we are in this picture! In August 1960 'Jubilee' 4-6-0 No 45659 *Drake* arrives at Leicester on a Bradford to St Pancras express, in a picture that I'm sure you agree captures perfectly the young trainspotters perched above on those bridge girders, one of which might have been you! *Barry O. Hilton*

Great Central station, often travelling to London with his job. Sounds glamorous doesn't it? Well, not so much after he related the story of how he and other GC staff had been called out to help search for the missing head of a chap who had thrown himself in front of a train at Leicester. Having had no success it was eventually found several days later at the Central shed wedged behind an engine's cylinder block. No wonder I didn't join the railways!

Our last Great Central Club trip in 1961 was a Sunday visit at the beginning of December to the Shrewsbury area sheds, and the major railway junction town of Crewe, with its important depots and large locomotive works. This was an exciting place to visit for us youngsters; like Derby, it was then producing the new 'Peak' diesels, but thankfully still overhauling large numbers of steam engines including the 'Coronation' 'Pacifics'.

To underline in your *abc* the last member of any class you

Crewe Locomotive Works, 3 December 1961

Class	Number/Name
Preserved locos	3020 *Cornwall*, 790 *Hardwicke*, 0-4-0 1439, 0-4-0 *Pet*
0-6-0T 3F	47592, 47618 (Works locos)
0-6-0 2F	51446
0-6-0 3F	52218, 52312, 52441, 52459
0-6-0 4F	44088, 44249, 44365
4-6-0 Class 5	44686, 44690, 44743, 44746, 44753, 44756, 44765, 44787, 44890, 44942, 44943, 44949, 44983, 44989, 45092, 45096, 45101, 45107, 45145, 45183, 45200, 45201, 45215, 45228, 45236, 45256, 45262, 45301, 45337, 45386, 45421, 45429, 45493
0-6-0T 3F	47251, 47636
2-8-0 8F	48018, 48130, 48151, 48397, 48399, 48443, 48495, 48528, 48551, 48552, 48658, 48669, 48700, 48703, 48762
4-6-0 'Patriot'	45543 *Home Guard*
4-6-0 'Jubilee'	45570 *New Zealand*, 45645 *Collingwood*, 45646 *Napier*, 45680 *Camperdown*, 45695 *Minotaur*, 45702 *Colossus*, 45709 *Implacable*, 45710 *Irresistible*, 45719 *Glorious*,
4-6-0 'Royal Scot'	46109 *Royal Engineer*, 46133 *The Green Howards*
4-6-2 'Princess Coronation'	46223 *Princess Alice*, 46224 *Princess Alexandra*, 46253 *City of St Albans*
0-8-0 7F	49130, 49313, 49361, 49394, 49433
2-4-2T L&Y	50850 (withdrawn - the last of the class)

4-6-2 'Britannia'	70022 *Tornado*, 70026 *Polar Star*, 70042 *Lord Roberts*, 70043 *Lord Kitchener*, 70048 *The Territorial Army 1908-1958*, 70049 *Solway Firth*
4-6-0 BR Class 5	73090
4-6-0 BR Class 4	75026
2-8-0 'WD'	90147, 90218, 90276, 90365
2-10-0 BR 9F	92016, 92017, 92018, 92025, 92076, 92083, 92129, 92133, 92159
BR Type 4	D1 *Scafell Pike*, D3 *Skiddaw*, D7 *Ingleborough*, D8 *Penyghent*
EE Type 4	D214, D231 *Sylvania*, D290, D298
BR Type 2	D5073

needed was always something special, so coming across my last 'Patriot', No 45544 *Home Guard*, at the works was brilliant. Having cleared the class, I then carried out an exercise to identify all the various places where I had 'copped' each one of these famous engines. The largest number was a surprising total of 17 having been recorded at Rugby, followed by ten at Leicester, eight at Nuneaton, four at Liverpool, three at Crewe, and the remainder at Birmingham, Carnforth, London, York, Warrington and Chester.

The number of 'Patriots' observed at Rugby surprises me now. On the basis that 17 were seen there for the first time back in 1961, my visits certainly were more frequent than I can account for. Sadly, those visit records have disappeared, unlike some of my memories, these including being allowed up on the footplate of crimson Stanier 'Pacific' No 46244 *King George VI* at the station, when she pulled in on a Euston-bound train. Also, having decided with the boys to stay later than normal one summer's evening, we were rewarded by seeing a then rare Scottish 'Britannia', No 70051 *Firth of Forth*, pass by on a non-stop northbound express. I even remember our cheering and celebrations on seeing her – it remains another great moment I treasure.

Staying with the West Coast route, on our visit to Crewe I also recorded some main-line electrics, which by then were working between Crewe and Manchester. My first ever sighting of them had actually occurred a few years before while enjoying a day's spotting at Nuneaton, when a freight hauled by an 8F passed through containing three or four of the new E3000 Type A electric locomotives in tow, after they had been on exhibition in the London area. As there was no hint of the electric wires in the area at the time, I was a surprise to see them. But now things were very different, as confirmed by one of the GC Club's newsletters, which reported that bases for the overhead gantries were in place in the vicinity of Watford, and overhead wiring erection was near Weedon approaching Nuneaton.

Returning to my old record books again, I proudly recorded on 23 December 1961 that my locomotive number collection had reached 8,000 with 8F freight engine No 48170. The total of locomotives seen was made up as follows:

Western Region	1,216
Eastern Region	923
London Midland Region	3,525
Southern Region	409
50721-58850 locos	85
BR Standard locos	791
Diesel locos	977
Electric locos	74

Among these numbers, my observation of named engines (my heroes!) totalled 1,010:

Western Region	393
Eastern Region	174
London Midland Region	343
Southern Region	54
Br Standard locos	46

As you can imagine, my quest to discover engines not seen before ('copped'), certainly in the Midland Region, was becoming more of a challenge, with express locomotives a real find, as I rarely came across them. But the good news was that I still retained my interest and enthusiasm for the hobby as we entered the New Year, which certainly didn't start quietly, with newspaper headlines proclaiming 'A New Year Freeze Up' and describing the heavy snow storms that struck in earnest on Sunday 31 December, affecting southern parts of England right through to Scotland. New Year's Day, unlike today, was a working day with a full British Railways service that bore the brunt of the chaos caused by the snow, which blocked many lines. In some areas frost was severe both day and night, causing freezing of points, water columns and heating apparatus, and resulting in electrical and mechanical signalling failures throughout the system.

The disruption caused by the severe weather lasted for a week, but every cloud has a silver lining, because it did result in steam locomotives replacing main-line diesels, many of which had failed on lots of routes. There was also the unexpected news of some stored 'Princess Royals' being returned to traffic on the West Coast Main Line. Closer to home, I think it's worth reminding ourselves about the 'good old days', when we enjoyed no central heating in our homes, and the scraping of frost from the inside of our bedroom windows was the norm during winter cold spells. Certainly our upstairs rooms in our house, including the bathroom, had no heating, which meant that you did well to put your legs more than half way down under the bedcovers because it felt so cold, and getting up in the morning was achieved very quickly!

But at least that Christmas period was quite exciting for me, because I had suddenly come into a lot of money for possibly the first time in my life. Had I won the pools? No, it came from the Christmas tips I received on my paper round as I wished my customers seasonal greetings. With more than 50 papers delivered I must have collected well over £30, a significant sum for me, and enough to allow me to think about planning a spotting trip to Scotland later in 1962. One thing it certainly helped me with was the purchase of a new camera, a Kodak Brownie 44A, which took 12 black and white pictures 44mm square (hence the name). I understand that it was the first camera to employ a plastic lens from Combined Optical Industries Ltd, using 'Perspex'. It was also fitted with two stops numbered 12 and 13, to allow some degree of control over the exposure, so no excuses now!

1962
(January to August)

Understandably the harsh winter weather restricted our trainspotting trips early on in the New Year, with just a few numbers recorded locally in Leicester, including one of an old Johnson 2Fs, No 58138, which I 'copped' on 15C on Saturday 6 January while she was on the way to Coalville depot to join up with her sister engines working on the West Bridge line. The following Saturday, the 13th, 'Britannia' No 70001 *Lord Hurcomb* was recorded together with two 'Peaks', Nos D43 and D127, both of which I hadn't seen before. On Saturday 27 January a couple more 'Peaks', Nos D120 and D151, were observed, as well as 8F No 48473 from Royston shed (55D), and Thompson 'B1' No 61182 from March (31B).

Our first Great Central Railway Society outing in 1962 was on Sunday 28 January and took us to eight sheds in the Derby and Nottingham areas, together with a return visit to Derby Locomotive Works. Compared with our previous trip to Crewe, this was rather dour, with named engines a rarity, the exception being at Burton shed (17B), to which a large number of 'Jubilee' engines had recently been transferred. Despite the large number of locomotives observed on the day I was now visiting sheds where I was recording very few 'cops', particularly locally, with none at Coalville, despite 21 locomotives being present, six out of 62 at Toton, 14 from 75 at Kirby-in-Ashfield, none at Westhouses out of 35, and eight from 89 at Nottingham (16A). Only Colwick shed (40E) saved the day, with 46 new locomotives noted out of the 95 recorded on shed. Looking back at our trip I was struck by the large numbers of freight engines observed, particularly the 40-odd 8F 2-8-0s observed at one depot alone, Kirby-in-Ashfield, which served the Nottinghamshire coalfield.

Burton-on-Trent (17B), 28 January 1962

Class	Number/Name
2-6-0 5MT	42764, 42769, 42818, 42822, 42825, 42829, 42873
4-6-0 Class 5	45348
0-6-0 3F	43608, 43637, 43669, 43689
0-6-0 4F	43793, 44124, 44151, 44435, 44436, 44439, 44552, 44458, 44538
4-6-0 'Jubilee'	45557 *New Brunswick*, 45561 *Saskatchewan*, 45579 *Punjab*, 45585 *Hyderabad*, 45615 *Malay States*, 45617 *Mauritius*, 45626 *Seychelles*, 45636 *Uganda*, 45650 *Blake*, 45712 *Victory*
0-4-0ST 0F	47000
0-6-0T 3F	47313, 47438, 47464, 47641, 47645
2-8-0 8F	48165
0-8-0 7F	49323
4-6-0 BR Class 4	75061
2-8-0 'WD'	90480
4-6-0 'B1'	61068
2-8-0 'O4'	63616
Diesel shunters	D2856, D3569, D3570, D3571, D3572, D3585

Kirkby-in-Ashfield (16B)

2-6-2T Class 3	40073, 40088, 40089, 40099, 40115, 40124, 40136, 40168, 40175 40182, 40184, 40186, 40195
0-6-0 1F	41844
2-6-2T Class 4	42080, 42222, 42231, 42232, 42618
0-6-0T 3F	47317

0-6-0 4F	43885, 43903, 43933, 43941, 43972, 44091, 44202, 44252, 44416, 44418, 44470
2-8-0 8F	48001, 48003, 48004, 48006, 48011, 48088, 48092, 48096, 48097, 48098, 48100, 48114, 48119, 48137, 48156, 48173, 48182, 48192, 48214, 48215, 48219, 48223, 48224, 48225, 48267, 48272, 48277, 48282, 48315, 48334, 48379, 48392, 48395, 48405, 48442, 48541, 48553, 48611, 48621, 48673, 48693
2-6-0 BR Class 2	78013
2-8-0 'WD'	90002

It occurs to me that one thing I haven't described yet was what it was like visiting these large steam sheds, which contained all the necessary facilities to service and maintain locomotives including water columns, ash pits, washout points, coaling facilities and water towers. So what better place to start than on our coach arriving at our destination, everyone on board excitedly grabbing their notepads, pens and *abc*s ready to invade the shed. But first there must be patience, as our Club's secretary, Tony Moore, enters the Depot Foreman's office with the all-important shed pass, emerging after a short while with a wave as the signal for us to jump off the coach and join him. Entering the shed yard first, we are met with rows and rows of locomotives, some cold and dead, others simmering, awaiting a future duty. Just imagine those 8Fs I mentioned standing there towering above us as we make our way down the running lines, dodging the hot coke braziers guarding the shed's water columns to ensure the water supply doesn't freeze. Everywhere on the ground is the debris of railway operation, pools of dirty water, chunks of coal, large piles of ash, old wooden sleepers, a jumble of metal tools and oil cans. As we dive into the shed's dark depths the yellow glow from poor lighting barely identifies our prey as we follow one another down

'Jubilee' No 45615 *Malay States* at Burton shed on 28 January 1962. *Tony Moore* the narrow lines that separate the locomotives. Excited shouts come from those lads at the front as they come across a 'cop', you busy scribbling down the valuable numbers, mindful of your targets, the ones you need to see, and the reason you've travelled so far that day.

The smell of sulphur lingers in the building as you pat the tender of Kirby's 8F No 48097, the last engine that you need from its allocation. Now you know how Stanley felt meeting Doctor Livingstone – the elation, it was all worth it – and now the bragging can begin – surely no one else could have cleared 16B!

Back on the coach, as we leave out come our spotters' books for a quick check on the numbers taken, and soon crosses and ticks cover the notepad's list of engine numbers you've collected, and there was even time to cab a 'Standard', No 78013, as she stood in the yard in light steam, another fact that needs to be recorded. Someone moans that there were no 'namers' on shed, but you don't care thanks to that very dirty freight locomotive No 48097 – the quest continues, but now elsewhere.

I mentioned earlier the AC electric passenger service operating between Crewe and Manchester. A new development that January saw the Crewe to Liverpool line electrified, and with work well under way on the West Coast Main Line to the south as far as Stafford, modernisation of all aspects of railway operation had accelerated since 1960, and in large areas of the rail network diesel and electric locomotives had become established as the chief form of express motive power, including sadly on the Midland main line through Leicester, with 'Peak' diesels taking over a lot of the passenger traffic from steam. My observations at the 'Birdcage' at this time still recorded occasional steam express power, but sadly spotting there was quickly losing its appeal for me compared to the Great Central line, where thankfully most of the passenger and freight traffic was still steam-hauled. I was beginning to realise that if I was to continue to witness steam in regular action locally, perhaps the GC was going to be the place to go.

Of course we were now growing up in the 'Swinging Sixties',

The 'Birdcage', Leicester, 1962. *Leicester Mercury*

and around this time we discovered a new thing called 'pop music', thanks to a commercial radio station that broadcast on the 208 metres medium wave frequency, called Radio Luxembourg. You only could listen to it in the evenings, which we did by tuning in on our transistor radios while waiting for the evening's 'Grimsby Fish' to arrive at the Great Central station.

I remember that we got it into our heads that because the radio station was coming from abroad it was illegal to listen to it, so we felt we were revolting against the establishment if we did. Certainly it was different. We had never heard commercials broadcast before and, as if to confirm that it was a little dodgy, the BBC never mentioned its existence, and our Mums and Dads dismissed it, so its popularity with us young teenagers was guaranteed.

Our interest in 'pop' perhaps suggests that we were growing up fast. I certainly thought I was as, despite the cold weather, for me romance was in the air, when I plucked up enough courage to ask out a young lady who lived next door to Big Stu. It was my first ever date and I was out to impress, so where on your very first date do you take the lovely Pauline to impress her? Well, certainly not down the railway. Instead, why not to see a very popular TV couple of the time, Pearl Carr and Teddy Johnson, in concert at the De Montfort Hall in Leicester? Obviously I'd like to report that Pauline couldn't resist me, but she did; it showed that I certainly knew more about trains than about young ladies. But never mind, I was pleased because I didn't really want to two-time Hayley, so quickly let's get back to my other passion.

In February 1962 our second Great Central Railway Society trip destination was the Birmingham area on Sunday the 18th, which saw us visit 12 sheds and the former Great Western Railway works at Wolverhampton, and for the first time saw my new Kodak 44A camera in action. A report about the Birmingham trip appeared later in the GC Club's Spring Review, reminding me that these were the days before the vast 'Spaghetti Junction' on the M6 had been built, so consequently the article described Bescot shed (21B) as situated in the middle of a wide vacant space in the centre of a built-up area.

No 6006 *King George I* at Wolverhampton Stafford Rd shed on 18 February 1962.

On my visit there we also came across two badly damaged wagons lying by the side of the track following a derailment.

The article also clears up for me which of the area's shed it was that was adjacent to a race course, after I'd remembered climbing up a slope and looking down onto it. Surprisingly, my mystery shed was Oxley, to which I refer later. On a sadder note, I was shocked soon after our visit to learn that the subject of my 'King' photograph at Wolverhampton Stafford Road (84A), No 6006 *King George I*, was withdrawn from service just ten days afterwards on 28 February, and scrapped at Swindon the following month.

Wolverhampton Stafford Road (84A), 18 February 1962	
Class	**Number/Name**
4-6-0 'County'	1002 *County of Berks*, 1016 *County of Hants*
0-6-0PT '1600'	1639
2-6-2T '4500'	2248, 2287
2-6-2T '5100'	4120, 5152, 5183, 5199
4-6-0 'Castle'	5011 *Tintagel Castle*, 5015 *Kingswear Castle*, 5031 *Totnes Castle*, 5045 *Earl of Dudley*, 5046 *Earl of Cawdor*, 5047 *Earl of Dartmouth*, 7012 *Barry Castle*, 7029 *Clun Castle*
0-6-2T '5600'	6627
0-6-0PT '5700'	3615, 3778
4-6-0 'King'	6005 *King George II*, 6006 *King George I*, 6007 *King William III*, 6008 *King James II*, 6014 *King Henry VII*, 6020 *King Henry IV*
4-6-0 'Hall'	5958 *Knolton Hall*, 5960 *Saint Edmund Hall*
4-6-0 'Modified Hall'	6987 *Shervington Hall*, 7928 *Wolf Hall*
0-6-0T '6400'	6418
4-6-0 'Grange'	6856 *Stowe Grange*

2-8-0 8F	48460
2-6-0 BR Class 2	78008
0-6-0PT '9400'	8426, 8498, 9420
Oxley (84B)	
0-6-0PT '1600'	1650
0-6-0 '2251'	3200
2-8-0 '2800'	2856, 3802, 3810
2-8-0T '4200'	5259
4-6-0 'Hall'	4903 *Astley Hall*, 4906 *Bradfield Hall*, 4912 *Berrington Hall*, 4966 *Shakenhurst Hall*, 4973 *Sweeney Hall*, 4984 *Albrighton Hall*, 5902 *Howick Hall*, 5916 *Trinity Hall*, 5919 *Worsley Hall*, 5930 *Hannington Hall*, 5953 *Dunley Hall*, 5985 *Mostyn Hall*, 5996 *Mytton Hall*, 6904 *Charfield Hall*, 6935 *Browsholme Hall*
4-6-0 'Modified Hall'	6963 *Throwley Hall*, 6975 *Capesthorne Hall*, 6994 *Baggrave Hall*, 7911 *Lady Margaret Hall*
0-6-2T '5600'	5606, 5658
0-6-0PT '5700'	4626, 4683, 8753, 9768
2-8-2T '7200'	7213, 7218
4-6-0 'Grange'	6817 *Gwenddwr Grange*, 6851 *Hurst Grange*, 6854 *Roundhill Grange*, 6870 *Bodicote Grange*, 6871 *Bourton Grange*
0-6-0PT '9400'	8428, 8435, 9479
2-6-2T BR Class 3	82041
Diesel shunters	D3035 D3036, D3037 D3039 D3752 D3757

On revisiting my trip records it surprises me how much I'd forgotten. To discover that I had visited Kidderminster during this trip in BR days prior to the establishment of the Severn Valley Railways came as a surprise, also that Stratford-upon-Avon had been a small sub-shed. Embarrassingly, I had no recollection of going round Oxley shed at Wolverhampton, despite observing a staggering 19 'Hall' Class locomotives there, which, when you added the seven 'Grange' locomotives, outnumbered the other engines observed which didn't carry nameplates. Just imagine that today, if you could see such a spectacle at what wasn't a very high-profile engine shed, yet back then what I witnessed was perhaps just a normal Sunday. Incidentally, by now I had concluded that the scrapping of my favourite steam locomotives was all his fault, of course – Dr Richard Beeching – who had been appointed Chairman of the British Railways Board in 1961.

Now, I wouldn't like to pretend I was mature enough at my age to be a political expert, nor that I took much notice that the railways were losing vast amounts of money, as its passenger and freight traffic declined, but did we really have a Minister of Transport, a certain Mr Marples, in charge then who also just happened to be a director of a major road-building business. It beggar's belief! It's a fact that my generation were taught to respect our elders, especially those in power, and not to challenge anyone in authority. They were in charge and knew what was best for us and the country, including the reshaping of British Railways, which as we now know would lead to the wholesale closure of what were considered little-used and unprofitable railway lines, the removal of stopping passenger trains and the closure of local stations on the lines that remained open.

Now, I'm getting far too serious for my little tale of a young trainspotter, so back to the 1960s. Just a week after our Birmingham visit, I was to venture out again to Peterborough and March. This trip proved different, as I went out all on my own, perhaps for the first time leaving my friends behind. I'm glad to say that everything went well, and once again I managed to visit both New England and March sheds. I enjoyed the experience, and was quite comfortable with my own company despite the late-afternoon weather bringing some snow showers. Being a Sunday visit, New England certainly delivered more engines on shed, with more than 20 of the Standard 9F 2-10-0s observed, and a similar number of 'Austerity' 'WDs'. There were also a large number of Gresley 'V2s' and Thompson 'B1s' present. My 'Pacific' interest centred on a King's Cross 'A4', No 60029 *Woodcock*, which was a great 'cop' for me.

March shed was packed with both diesels and steam of various classes from the old Great Eastern 0-6-0 'J15s' and 'J17s' to the latest Brush Type 2 diesels to enter service. The highlight for me was coming across 'Britannia' 'Pacific' No 70000 *Britannia* among the ten class members present, having just been transferred from Norwich. It was the first time I had seen her, and a 'cop' well worth boasting about when I met the boys at school the following day.

My journey to Peterborough that Sunday was again by train, this time steam-hauled with BR Standard No 75040 being in charge of my local from Leicester. I remember it was always exciting approaching Peterborough, as our line ran adjacent to the East Coast Main Line for quite a distance, which encouraged me to hang out of an open carriage window in the hope of seeing our train run parallel with an East Coast express. I certainly treasured one particular moment when 'A4' No 60034 *Lord Faringdon* overhauled my train on this stretch of line one lovely summer's morning later in the year. If you have ever seen *Elizabethan Express*, the famous British Transport film, I believe that part of the filming of 'A4' No 60017 *Silver Fox* at speed, one of the most exciting bits, was done in this area.

Looking at my records I was still keen to see the 'Deltics', and was rewarded with observing four of them passing through, including the newly named No D9007 *Pinza*. I don't know who it was at BR responsible for picking the names eventually allocated to the class, but you've got to hand it to them – the decision to use racehorses was brilliant, and further enhanced their image for speed and power.

March (31B), Sunday 25 February 1962	
Class	**Number/Name**
2-6-4T Class 4	42062, 42577
0-6-0 4F	44521, 44571
4-6-0 Class 5	44810, 44938, 45260
4-6-0 'Jubilee'	45641 *Sandwich*
2-6-2 'V2'	60872 *King's Own Yorkshire Light Infantry*, 60925
2-6-0 'K4'	62021, 62038, 62039, 62051, 62066, 62067, 62068, 62070
4-6-0 'B1'	61003 *Gazelle*, 61043, 61048, 61052, 61054, 61059, 61095, 61142, 61171, 61182, 61203, 61204, 61205, 61233, 61252, 61253, 61322
2-6-0 'K3'	61834, 61840, 61886, 61890, 61896, 61915, 61929, 61954
2-8-0 'O2'/'O4'	63669, 63678, 63687, 63705, 63725, 63786, 63818, 63868, 63878, 63887, 63890, 63899, 63922, 63934, 63938, 63946, 63962, 63973
0-6-0 'J6'	64253
0-6-0 'J20'	64687, 64691
0-6-0 'J15'	65420
0-6-0 'J17'	65541, 65560, 65576, 65578, 65586
2-6-0 BR Class 4	76030, 76031, 76034
4-6-2 'Britannia'	70000 *Britannia*, 70001 *Lord Hurcomb*, 70002 *Geoffrey Chaucer*, 70005 *John Milton*, 70006 *Robert Burns*, 70008 *Black Prince*, 70009 *Alfred the Great*, 70011 *Hotspur*, 70013 *Oliver Cromwell*, 70030 *William Wordsworth*
2-6-0 BR Class 4	76030, 76031, 76034

2-8-0 'WD'	90003, 90038, 90224, 90259, 90279, 90438, 90498, 90646
2-10-0 BR 9F	92192
Diesel shunters	15002, 12136, D2013, D2016, D2201, D2240, D3065, D3337, D3491 D3493
EE Type 4	D259
BR Type 2	D5038, D5041
EE Type 3	D6723
Brush Type 2	D5508 D5520, D5538 D5542, D5545, D5552, D5556 D5559 D5561 D5568, D5572, D5573, D5582, D5586, D5588, D5600, D5621, D5668
BTH Type 1	D8215, D8216, D8219

Around this time a train through Leicester was to become the focal point of my trainspotting over the next year or so. Surprisingly it wasn't a glamorous express – in fact, quite the opposite, because it contained smelly fish! The train, the 4.30pm 'Fish' from the East Coast port of Grimsby to Whitland in South Wales, was routed down the Great Central through Leicester Central, where it stopped each weekday evening around 8.15pm to change its engine crew and for the locomotive to take on water. I began to record seeing the train in March 1962 soon after news reached us that 40E, Immingham depot, had started to use its recently allocated 'Britannias' to haul it. A number of the 'Brits' had just been transferred away from East Anglia to the East Coast, including a number unseen before by yours truly, so it was only natural that I joined the lads, cycling down there after my paper round, tea and homework, to wait for the arrival of the 'Fish'. On close inspection of the fish train, one thing I remember was not only the smell, but the water dripping from its wagons. I never had the opportunity to see inside one, but I'm sure there was no such thing as refrigerated wagons in those days, so you can imagine that quite a lot of ice was packed in the white wagons to preserve the valuable cargo on its journey south, and what I was witnessing of course was it melting.

Yes, the 'Fish' had become the 'star turn' for us on the Great Central, but I mustn't forget the regular Annesley to Woodford freights hauled by Annesley 9F 2-10-0s. These trains were the outstanding feature of the line at the time, with their 9Fs

The 'Fish' arriving at Leicester Central with No 70037 in charge.

regularly hauling up to 60 loose-coupled mineral wagons of coal or steel, and were to be seen operating all through the day and night. It's funny, after observing these freights over the years, how one single occasion can stand out. Mine was on a cold winter's evening when I was walking with friends down Blackbird Road on the way to the Leicester Speedway. Suddenly a 9F stormed by on the nearby raised embankment heading north with its long rake of mineral wagons, a bright glow from its firebox lighting up the locomotive's cab in the dark night, and sparks flying up from its chimney. It was gone in seconds but for me never forgotten.

Despite not having a 'Birdcage', the lads and I soon discovered a couple of good meeting points down the GC to await the arrival of the 'Fish'. The first was a piece of land accessed through a gate at the bottom of the cobbled Talbot Lane adjacent to the Jewry Wall Museum and the Vaughan College area just south of the Great Central station. On the other side of the College on Castle Walk was an elevated area on which a public seating bench had been erected by the City Council. It's positioning was, I assume, because it overlooked Leicester's famous Roman Jewry Wall site. During the summer months it became the perfect place for us to hang around and socialise, being close enough to give us a great view of the passing railway traffic in the distance. Meeting up regularly down there saw our enthusiasts' group grow, with a number of lads including Doug Combey and his brother Mick from our estate joining us, together with Keith Mapley and John Kempin, who brought with them a large group of friends from the Great Central Club. Very soon our regular evening meetings developed into our version of a youth club – open-air, of course. We were all drawn there at first because of trains, together with pop as we regularly listened to music on 208 Radio Luxembourg, and, dare I say, showing a growing shared interest in a new subject, young ladies.

Perhaps for the first time I also began to experience that very human feeling of envy, after some of my new friends began turning up on their flashy racing bikes, making my straight-handlebar Palm Beach cycle begin to look very unfashionable – all of a sudden appearances were starting to matter. Yes, back then your status in the group was measured by what bicycle you owned, a lightweight frame being an essential requirement, and at 15, with hormones raging, no longer was I prepared to trail behind the 'Claud Butlers', 'Mercians' and 'Freddie Grubbs' of my trainspotting friends. I was determined not to be left behind, and couldn't wait any longer, so my planned trip to Scotland later that year, for which I had been saving up since Christmas, was sacrificed to provide funds for a new racing bike.

Locally we had Sid Mottram Cycles on Narborough Road, where not only were the bikes an attraction, but also Mr Mottram's two young daughters, who helped in his shop, and I'm sure it encouraged a couple of the lads to purchase his bikes, but I needed a racer type that was different, to make my mark with my growing band of friends. The result was a 'Geo Evans' with a 531 tubing frame, sprint wheels, centre pull brakes and campagnola gears, painted in enamel green, not far from the Brunswick Green BR used for express locomotives. It was stunning! Although it cost around £48, and subsequently my Post Office savings book was decimated, strange to say it gave me more satisfaction to pick up my new purchase from Mr Evans's cycle shop on Humberstone Road than any car I've purchased since. I was so proud of it that I kept it upstairs in my bedroom for ages and cleaned it whenever I used it in wet weather until Mum read the Riot Act. Later, when a parent myself, I could understand her point, but at the time it was my pride and joy.

Our next GC Society trip in March was to the Manchester area, which turned out to be another marathon, when we managed to visit 15 sheds as well as the railway works at Horwich in a single day, observing more than 400 locomotives. Such was the interest in this trip, because so many boys wanted to go, that the Club ran two coaches for the first time. For many of the sheds it was my first visit, so I particularly enjoyed going around Newton Heath (26A), where among the large number of 4-6-0 'Black 5s' were two of the named members, Nos 45154 *Lanarkshire Yeomanry* and 45156 *Ayrshire Yeomanry*, together with a good sprinkling of 'Jubilees' and 'Royal Scots'.

A couple of old Midland 4-4-0 '2Ps', Nos 40453 and 40681, both still in service, caught my attention at Patricroft shed (26F), which also contained ten members of the 4-6-0 BR Standard Class 5s. It had always been ambition to visit the ex-Great Central shed at Gorton, which held an even number of both Midland and Eastern locomotives as well as providing a glimpse through the railings of Bo-Bo electric No 26000 *Tommy* in the works yard. Further highlights for me included catching up with Leicester Central 'B1' No 61008 *Kudu* at Agecroft shed, where it shared its home base with the small L&Y dock tanks, one of which I managed to photograph. Horwich Works still retained some old Lancashire & Yorkshire Railway tank engines for works duties, but on the down side I have to say that visits on the way back to Bolton, Wigan and Warrington were getting rather familiar, with only a handful of locomotives observed for the first time.

Agecroft (26B), Sunday 18 March 1962	
Class	**Number/Name**
4-6-0 'B1'	61008 *Kudu* (ex-Leicester GC, 15E), 61298, 61369, 61273 (passed by)
2-6-4T Class 4	42474, 42646, 42647
2-6-0 5MT	42724, 42726, 42753, 42819, 42868, 42891
4-6-0 Class 5	44792, 44823, 44928, 44929, 45261, 45337
4-6-0 'Jubilee'	45584 *North West Frontier*, 45599 *Bechuanaland*, 45607 *Fiji*
0-6-0T 3F	47224, 47574, 47578, 47579
0-8-0 7F	49618 (withdrawn), 49668
0-4-0ST 0F	51206, 51207, 51237
0-4-0ST 2F	51408
2-8-0 'WD'	90110, 90274, 90292, 90307, 90354, 90359, 90372, 90546, 90558, 90564, 90632, 90679
Horwich Works	
0-6-0T 3F	47402 47429
0-6-0ST 2F	11368 11304, 11324, *Wren*, 1008
2-6-0 5MT	42742, 42761, 42772, 42817, 42828, 42865, 42981
2-6-0 4MT	43070
0-6-0 4F	43988, 44397, 44028, 44061, 44078, 44086, 44152, 44169, 44221, 44334, 44346, 44403, 44405, 44467, 44550, 44592
0-6-0T 3F	47550

Horwich Works continued	
Class	**Number/Name**
2-8-0 8F	48169, 48321, 48462, 48631, 48685, 48686, 48756
New-built shunters	D4122, D4123, D4124, D4125, D4126, D4127, D4128, D4129
Scrap line	diesel 12001; steam 40132, 40180, 43863, 51336, 52429

One lasting impression from the trip was how neat and tidy we found the loco works at Horwich, with lawns and gardens within its grounds. It was so clean it was difficult to believe that it was a loco repair facility.

Dock tank No 51206 at Agecroft shed.

Horwich Works shunters Nos 11368 and 11324.

Back in Leicester, one Saturday morning in April Big Stu and I joined eight other members of our railway club for a ride on the old Leicester to Swannington railway in a brake van of a freight train, the 11.45am from Leicester to Desford Junction. This was the line I mentioned earlier, on which the Johnson 2F 0-6-0s operated the freight service I enjoyed seeing on my paper round as it made its way out of the city each evening towards Glenfield.

One thing we didn't anticipate was that, despite the train being a freight-only service, our trip was sanctioned with the condition that our party obtained passenger tickets for the journey, with instructions received that morning to pick them up from the London Road station ticket office. This led to one of older lads dashing off on his racing bike to obtain them as our train waited. Despite our last-minute panic, the locomotive crew and guard seemed very relaxed while waiting at the line's West Bridge wharf terminus, perhaps reflecting the fact that the service on the line consisted of only two trains daily.

Tickets finally secured, we joined the freight train of 39 empty wagons for the trip to Desford. Our train's motive power was No 58137 of Coalville shed (15E), a vintage engine whose survival into the 1960s was no doubt down to its ability to operate through the very narrow bore of the Glenfield Tunnel, which, despite being more than a mile long, was well known to us lads thanks to our adventures during school holidays exploring it, and especially when trying to get the girls to go further in than a few yards!

Incidentally, the West Bridge terminus with its marshalling yards covered quite an area behind terraced houses just round the corner from my grandparents' home on Vaughan Street, a very famous place because of my birth there (sadly no blue plaque has yet been erected by the City Council). Besides my railway interest in the line, I was aware of a family connection with it after my Grandad Dennis told me that his father, John Allen, had owned a coal business that operated from the wharf; knowing little else, I imagined great-grandad running a large operation supplying his customers in the city with coal brought to the terminus by rail from the coalfields in north-east Leicestershire. Many years later, thanks once again to my family history research, I discovered that, yes indeed, there was a family coal business, which in December 1924 was sold by my grandfather's brother George to none other than my other great-grandfather Marling Lane for £50, therefore keeping it in the family. This was confirmed by another relation of mine, who was kind enough to let me have a copy of the receipt for the transaction, which reveals the scale of the business, the assets being purchased for £50 included a pony, with trolley and harness. I also learned that, sadly for great-grandad Marling, the business soon failed because of the refusal of customers to pay for the coal supplied to them; however, he did enjoy taking my great-grandmother out for rides into the Leicestershire countryside, which I though was nice, especially after finding out that the coal business empire wasn't quite what I had imagined.

When our journey eventually started, our freight made its way down the single-track line at 5mph over the Fosse Road bridge, and climbed through a large allotment area and over the

Into Glenfield Tunnel! *Colin Walker*

small level crossing on which stood the old Midland Railway signs. Climbing out of the city and passing our housing estate, we soon approached Robert Stephenson's Glenfield Tunnel; before entering the guard advised us to cover our mouths with handkerchiefs because of the smoky conditions in the small bore. Of course, we loved it, larking about in the guard's van in the dark with Big Stu pretending he was choking before taking massive gulps of fresh air again as we came out and approached the level crossing in Glenfield village, waving at the traffic patiently waiting for us to pass.

At Glenfield station we got off the guard's van to allow the engine to remove three wagons from the train and shunt them into a siding. We then set off up a steep gradient to Groby Junction, where a private line to a quarry branched off. A number of full wagons from the quarry were attached to our train after being shunted into position by the quarry's apple-green Hunslet 0-4-0 saddle tank. We then set off again climbing towards Ratby, then on to Desford Junction, where we left the freight in the yard and walked back towards the station to catch a train back to Leicester on the Burton branch line. Far removed from the hustle and bustle of the main rail network, I can't help thinking what a lovely job it must have been for the railwaymen to take their train with its ancient engine daily down this country line, with its footplate crew so familiar with local villagers to be on chatting terms as it slowly plodded on towards its journey's end at Desford.

My record for our return journey from Desford, a typical country station, indicates that we observed Coalville's 8F No 48619, no doubt on freight duties from the local coalfields, before joining our passenger train back to Leicester Midland, which was hauled by BR Standard Class 4 No 75058. On the way into the city our train passed over the raised embankment overlooking the Great Central shed (15D), where I noted its allocation of Gresley 'V2' 2-6-2 Nos 60815 and 60863 in the yard together with a withdrawn Midland tank engine, No 40167. A couple more engines noted on the GC that day were York 'B16' 4-6-0 No 61472 and No 70045 *Lord Rowallan*, one of the 'Britannias' recently transferred to Neasden shed in London.

Our Leicester observations continued that month with the sighting of Immingham 'Britannia' No 70037 *Hereward the Wake* on the 'Fish' on Wednesday evening, 11 April. The following Saturday a bike ride down the Midland resulted in us spotting sister engine No 70028 *Royal Star*, a former Western Region locomotive. Sunday 14 April saw me record two 'Jubilees', Nos 45622 *Nyasaland* and 45641 *Sandwich*, in the Midland shed yard, together with 'Royal Scot' No 46160 *Queen Victoria's Rifleman*, and a passing express produced one of the recently named Type 4 English Electric diesels, No D212 *Aureol*. Another 'Jubilee', No 45739 *Ulster* of Leeds Holbeck shed, was observed on Thursday

26th together with it Ivatt 2-6-0 No 43021 of Nuneaton depot, which, although local, I hadn't seen before.

By the end of April we were aware that the Great Central Railway Society had organised its second weekend trip away, this time to the North East area and Carlisle. Naturally we were keen to go as we had never visited the North Eastern sheds, and Carlisle still retained its magic for us young spotters. Permission from parents was now a formality, with my Mum and Dad feeling particularly sorry for me at the time following my major bicycle accident, which sadly did nothing to enhance my young ego, especially after the recent purchase of my new 'Geo Evans' racer. How I survived, I don't know. Well, I do really – I just wanted to extract a little sympathy from you the reader before describing the circumstances.

My new racer was geared for speed. No longer was I restricted to just three gears, thanks to additional ones that enhanced my bike's performance, soon demonstrated to the boys, with me often leaving them behind in my wake as we cycled down to the Central or the 'Birdcage'. Now, as you might know, the cycling position on a racer involves gripping the handlebars lower down, allowing you to lift your posterior to increase the leg power on the pedals. This helps you accelerate and increase your speed, and sometimes when doing so your head is down for a few seconds as you sprint forward. So there I was one evening just after leaving Big Stu's house, when I decided to accelerate in the manner described above, with head down. I went for it, imagining I was an 'A4' 'Pacific' storming through Grantham, when suddenly I found myself lying inside a car that I hadn't noticed parked by the roadside. I had gone head-first straight through its rear window, and found myself in a heap on the back seat. Extracting myself a few moments later through the car's shattered window, I couldn't understand why the car owner, who had heard a bang and had come to investigate, was so upset. After all, it was only a small window, whereas my bike's front wheel was no longer round and my front forks were bent backwards.

Seriously, though, those were the days when we didn't wear cycle helmets, so I can't help but think someone must have been looking after me. I was very lucky, sustaining only small cuts and scratches from glass splinters in my face and neck. My real injury, as mentioned earlier, was to my pride. When word got around about the circumstances of my accident, boy, did I take some stick, especially after my old Palm Beach bike was pressed back into service while my 'Geo Evans' was repaired.

Thank goodness I had the North East trip to look forward to, and my one-date ex-girlfriend Pauline, on hearing of my awful accident, gave me a kiss when I turned up at Big Stu's house to join the boys for the weekend. She was obviously glad to see I was still alive, and I'm sure there was a tear in her eye as we left to catch the coach. I thought my luck was in, but for some reason when I returned she seemed to have lost interest.

Why mention this? Well, 50 years later I was thrilled to discover an old black and white negative that pictured Pauline and I having a hug just before I departed on that weekend. I quickly had it developed so I could tell my old trainspotting pal Big Stu all about it; after all, he had lived next door to her. Full of excitement I rang my dear friend to give him the news, only to hear him giggle and reveal a secret that he had kept from me over all those years – at the time, unknown to me, she was more interested in him. The swine!

As luck would have it we had all been on our Easter school holidays during the week prior to our weekend away, so when news reached us on the morning of our departure, Friday 27 April, that a very special visitor had appeared at Leicester shed (15C) we had time to dash down to the 'Birdcage' to catch sight of 'Clan' 'Pacific' No 72006 *Clan Mackenzie* standing in the yard. Now a 'Clan' was a complete rarity at Leicester, so her sudden appearance caused a sensation within the local railway fraternity, with enthusiasts flocking throughout the day in large numbers to see her. Incidentally, she was in the company of 'Britannia' No 70005 *John Milton*, an engine we would bump into the following day.

The appearance of the 'Clans' was certainly the main topic of conversation as we left Leicester that late afternoon on the coach to travel up to York, where we were to stay overnight. On arrival we were delighted to find that our B&B was situated quite close to York's famous station, so, despite the late hour, we decided to pay a visit, which proved very rewarding with the sight of two 'A4' 'Pacifics', Nos 60003 *Andrew K. McCosh* and 60030 *Golden Fleece*, passing through, together with 'A3' *Cameronian*, which I copped, and two Deltics, Nos D9002 and D9020. It was also a very busy period for freight traffic, with 'B16' 4-6-0 No 61444 appearing, followed by 'K3' No 61846, and 'V2' No 60803 arriving on a mail train, to be replaced by English Electric Type 4 No D239, which took the service south.

Returning around midnight to our lodgings, the four of us – Big Stu, Stan, Colin Field, and me – once again found ourselves sharing the same bedroom. This not surprisingly resulted in us having very little sleep, and at around 4.00am the lure of York station proved too much for us, so we crept out of our boarding house and, by the time dawn was breaking, found ourselves once again back on its platforms. I remember it was a lovely morning, and despite the lack of sleep I was enjoying being with my pals, especially after experiencing a great 'cop' with my first ever sighting of Gateshead's 'A4' No 60018 *Sparrow Hawk*, whose appearance we gleefully reported to other lads from our party, who had missed her when they eventually caught up with us later on the platforms. This was a bit of brilliant one-upmanship, we thought, which sadly didn't last long as we came across her later on shed at York.

Our early start also give us the opportunity to visit the small engine shed at the south end of York station, which contained two 'Pacifics', 'A1' No 60140 *Balmoral* and 'A2' No 60522 *Straight Deal*, both of which looked in excellent external condition yet surprisingly were in store, with the tell-tale rags over their chimneys. I was later glad to learn that both engines did in fact return to service for a few more years. A second 'A2' 'Pacific' noted that morning was No 60518 *Tehran*, which I also 'copped', and I remember some of us spent time watching her crew's preparations as she readied herself to depart north on a school special to Edinburgh, while others waved at the girls sitting in the carriages. She was followed not long after by 'Britannia' No

70005 *John Milton*, which took us by surprise turning up in York less than 24 hours after seeing her at Leicester Midland shed.

Around 8.00am we returned to our boarding house and had breakfast before assembling outside for our first official visit of the day to York shed (50A)

After leaving York we travelled north to Northallerton and its very small shed, which held just a couple of BR Standard

York (50A), Saturday 28 April 1962	
Class	**Number/Name**
Diesel shunters	D2265, D2270, D3071, D3313, D3720, D3874
EE Type 4	D282, D350, D354, D356, D359, D385
4-6-2 'A4'	60018 *Sparrow Hawk*
4-6-2 'A3'	60042 *Singapore*, 60073 *St Gatien*
4-6-2 'A1'	60121 *Silurian*, 60124 *Kenilworth*, 60126 *Sir Vincent Raven*, 60138 *Boswell*, 60150 *Willbrook*, 60153 *Flamboyant*, 60154 *Bon Accord*
4-6-2 'A2'	60512 *Steady Aim*, 60516 *Hycilla*, 60526 *Sugar Palm*
2-6-2 'V2'	60810, 60848, 60852, 60854, 60856, 60859, 60895, 60896, 60918, 60872 *King's Own Yorkshire Light Infantry*, 60935, 60941, 60945, 60947, 60954, 60963, 60968
4-6-0 'B1'	61020 *Gemsbok*, 61023 *Hirola*, 61031 *Reedbuck*, 61039 *Steinbok*, 61049, 61050, 61053 61071, 61084, 61121, 61240 *Harry Hinchcliffe*, 61276, 61291, 61319, 61337
4-6-0 'B16'	61421, 61435, 61437, 61439, 61448, 61453, 61467
2-6-0 'K3'	61847, 61915

2-6-0 'K1'	62046, 62056, 62057, 62063
2-8-0 'O4'	63733
0-6-0 'J17'	65890
4-6-2 'Britannia'	70005 *John Milton*, 70034 *Thomas Hardy*
2-6-0 BR Class 4	76024
2-6-0 BR Class 3	77012
2-8-0 'WD'	90026, 90031, 90156, 90202, 90293, 90612
2-10-0 BR 9F	92044, 92146, 92175, 92177
2-6-0 4MT	43071 43131
4-6-0 'Jubilee'	45602 *British Honduras*

As we left our boarding house I managed to take a picture of our group as we stood waiting for our coach. John Elliott is in the middle giving us all the latest national news, with my gang, Stan with glasses, Colin Field behind and 'Big Stu', always hogging the camera, surrounded by the other lads. Incidentally, the main news was that a couple of days earlier an American moon rocket, 'Ranger IV', had landed on the far side of the moon, but had failed to send back any pictures due to a technical fault. As this was the first time an unmanned spacecraft had successfully reached the moon, and we had been brought up on the radio programme *Journey into Space* and 'Dan Dare' comics, not forgetting the *Flash Gordon* films, no wonder we all looked interested.

2-6-0s, Nos 78011 and 78012. I photographed a couple of freights passing by on the avoiding line hauled by 2-8-0 'Austerity' No 90459 and BR Type 2 diesel No D5101.

Thornaby shed (51L) was our next destination, where I began collecting the numbers of various classes of steam locomotive that were alien to us, never having being seen in the East Midlands. Among them were a large number of Raven 'Q6' and 'Q7' 0-8-0s, which I thought were perhaps the Eastern's equivalent to our Midland 8F freight locomotives, and used on similar coalfield duties. Also present were some very old 0-6-0s of Class 'J26' and 'J27'. This area, like everywhere else, was receiving new diesels, which was evident in the form of a large number of Type 2s present, as well as the large number of diesel shunters, so it was bonus to find one of the 'J72' 0-6-0s, No 69016, in steam performing shed shunting duties around the yard.

Thornaby (51L)	
Class	**Number/Name**
2-6-2 'V2'	60806, 60901, 60915, 60916
4-6-0 'B1'	61034 *Chiru*, 61218, 61220, 61257, 61259
2-6-0 'K1'	62001
0-8-0 'Q6'	63349, 63355, 63364, 63366, 63369, 63371, 63371, 63374, 63375, 63399, 63409, 63426, 63428, 63445, 63452, 63459,
0-8-0 'Q7'	63461
0-6-0 'J39'	64706, 64730, 64758, 64857, 64821
0-6-0 'J26'	65743, 65755, 65756, 65757, 65768
0-6-0 'J27'	65790, 65859, 65884
2-6-2T 'V1'	67640
0-6-2T 'J72'	69007, 69016, 69017

2-8-0 'WD'	90022, 90027, 90047, 90048, 90072, 90090, 90098, 90273, 90377, 90408, 90451, 90457, 90506, 90517
Diesel shunters	D2069, D2076, D3134, D3138, D3142, D3148, D3149
BR Type 2	D5112, D5153, D5154, D5159, D5166, D5168, D5170, D5171, D5113
BRC&W Type 2	D5371, D5373, D5374, D5375, D5377, D5378

By early afternoon we had visited West Hartlepool shed and arrived at Darlington, first visiting the works, which, like Horwich, was producing new diesel shunters as well as carrying out steam engine repairs. On arrival we were given a very good guide who took us through the various buildings, where we soon realised that, despite a number of 'V2s' and 'B1s' being present, the 'Plant' was not overhauling any of the region's 'Pacific' locomotives, which was a disappointment. New-built shunters were recorded from D4163 up to D4172, and a few 'Peaks' and English Electric Type 4s were also receiving attention.

Our visit then continued by travelling to the North Road scrapyard, which, if my memory is correct, found us in an area well away from the works. It was a strange atmosphere walking between rows of locomotives in the open, including a number of 'B16' 4-6-0s, all awaiting their fate, and I was surprised that, although not supervised, none of us had any thought of removing any of the smokebox number plates for souvenirs, despite so many available.

You will see from my record that Darlington shed (51A) contained a large allocation, which makes me wonder how quickly we were going around these depots when you consider that we managed to visit a further seven sheds later that day. I do remember that it was often stressed not to linger on our visits, with the Club eventually imposing fines on those of the party who did not conform.

Darlington (51A), Saturday 28 April 1962

Class	Number/Name
2-6-2T Class 3	40190
2-6-4T Class 4	42083, 42477, 42553, 42639
2-6-0 Class 4	43050, 43056, 43070, 43072, 43075, 43099, 43101, 43102, 43129, 43131
2-6-0 Class 2	46475, 46494
2-6-0 'A3'	60061 *Pretty Polly*, 60091 *Captain Cuttle*
2-6-2 'V2'	60808, 60811, 60855, 60865, 60973
4-6-0 'B1'	61013 *Topi*, 61032 *Stembok*, 61237 *Geoffrey H. Kitson*, 61178, 61321, 61353, 61382
2-6-0 'K1'	62004, 62007, 62041, 62043, 62048, 62059
0-8-0 'Q6'	63351, 63395, 63420
0-8-0 'Q7'	63471
0-6-0 'J27'	65860
2-6-2T 'V1'/'V3'	67601, 67623 (WD), 67666 (WD), 67682
0-6-2T 'J72'	68695, 69002, 69018
0-6-0ST 'J94'	68010, 68011, 68014, 68024, 68035, 68037, 68040 68043, 68052 68060
2-6-0 BR Class 2	78015
2-8-0 'WD'	90011, 90014, 90016, 90068, 90081, 90082, 90155, 90172, 90300, 90373
2-10-0 BR 9F	92144, 92198
Diesel shunters	D2079, D2336, D2340, D2590, D2618, D4161
BR Type 4	D14
EE Type 4	D240

2-8-0 'WD'	90443 (passed by)
Darlington North Road scrapyard	
4-6-0 'B16'	61411, 61412, 61413, 61415, 61419, 61443, 61450, 61451, 61460
2-6-4T 'L1'	67707, 67739, 67750, 67752, 67753, 67775, 67799
0-6-0 'J26'	65741, 65751, 65763
0-6-0ST 'J94'	68054, 68064
0-6-2T 'J72'	68688, 68689, 68703, 68729, 68734
4-8-0T 'T1'	69921

GCRS members visiting the North Road scrapyard.

Anyway, we soon pulled up at West Auckland shed (51F), observing a couple of BR Standard Class 3 2-6-0s, Nos 77002 and 77005, before enjoying one of the day's highlights watching 9F 2-10-0 92063 fitted with Westinghouse air pumps, visible by gaps in the running board on the fireman's side, passing

Consett at the head of an iron-ore train banked by 'Q6' 0-8-0 No 63379. We learned later that the running of these ore trains on the heavily graded route to Consett depended on the delivery of ore to Tyne Dock by ship, with three trains in operation at normal times, taking 1hr 51min for westbound and 1hr 11min for eastbound, so I was delighted that we were able to time it perfectly to photograph one in action that Saturday afternoon.

One of the Tyne Dock-Consett iron-ore trains in action at Consett behind No 92063.

Leaving Consett, Tyne Dock (52H) was visited, followed by Sunderland (52G) and Percy Main (52E), then came our final destination, the two sheds at North and South Blyth, which, although recognised under one shed code (52F), were in fact in two locations separated by a river. Both sheds were built in the late 19th century to handle the huge growth in coal traffic in the area, with the second of the two, North Blyth, built to eliminate excessive locomotive movement. At the time of our visit they provided, together with the shed at Percy Main, the 'J27' 0-6-0s as motive power for the coal traffic from the local collieries at Lynemouth, Bedlington and Chopington.

The Blyth chain ferry.

Our visit to Blyth produced an unusual twist because we had to travel across the river between the two sheds on a chain-hauled ferry, with the Club generously paying the 1 penny crossing fare for all of us.

When at Blyth, I must mention the mechanics of the staiths, which were very tall timber structures onto which coal trains were propelled and their wagons brought to a halt above loading chutes, into which the load was dropped, falling into the holds of colliers moored alongside on the river below. Sadly all this, including the two sheds, has disappeared, but one thing I'm sure

The Blyth staiths.

was that the sight of those staiths dominating the river skyline as we collected our numbers around the sheds proved memorable, especially to a group of 15-year-olds from the Midlands who had never seen anything like quite like it before.

By the way, the base of north-side staiths at North Blyth were immortalised in the film *Get Carter* (1971) starring Michael Caine. Towards the end of the film he chases a man along the wooden walkway carrying a double-barrelled shotgun with the serious intent to kill him. Needless to say, he achieves his goal – after all, he is Michael Caine – sorry, 'Jack Carter'.

If you remember, our previous evening at York resulted in very little sleep for me, so, despite finding ourselves in dormitory accommodation that Saturday evening at a youth hostel at Whitley Bay, I enjoyed a perfect night's sleep in my bunk bed, completely oblivious to the noise of 30-odd boys with whom I shared the room. I woke fully refreshed and looking forward to the day and our return to Carlisle, this time on a Sunday, with the prospect of finding a lot more locomotives present than on our previous visit in 1961.

Before we get started, I must mention one of my major trainspotting disappointments – not being allowed around Gateshead shed (52A) that Sunday. True, we did observe 20 or so engines in its yards, together with Gresley 'A4' 'Pacifics' Nos 60005 *Sir Charles Newton* and 60020 *Guillemot* through the windows of the repair shop, while we patiently waited as our envoys went forward to seek permission to visit, having not

Heaton (52B), Sunday 29 April 1962

Class	Number/Name
4-6-2 'A4'	60013 *Dominion of Canada*
4-6-2 'A3'	60058 *Blair Athol*, 60083 *Sir Hugo*, 60088 *Book Law*
ES1 Brush Traction (1902)	26500
Diesel shunters	D2104, D2165, D3240, D3670, D3673, D3679
BR Type 4	D22, D37
EE Type 4	D243, D244, D247, D259, D263, D273, D364
4-6-2 'A1'	60137 *Redgauntlet*, 60142 *Edward Fletcher*, 60147 *North Eastern*, 60155 *Borderer*
2-6-2 'V2'	60802, 60805, 60818, 60831, 60836, 60878, 60886, 60891, 60904, 60907, 60922, 60932
4-6-0 'B1'	61308
0-6-0 'J39'	64814, 64855, 64864, 64886, 64910, 64921, 64926, 64942
2-6-2T 'V1'/'V3'	67637, 67641, 67651, 67652, 67654, 67658, 67659, 67673, 67687, 67689, 67690, 67691
0-6-2T 'J72'	69008, 69021

obtained the magical 'permit'. Sadly, the answer came back 'No'. We were all gutted, so close but so far away, and I left, never ever to return – never was I to see two or three of the depot's famous 'A4s', which may have been there just a few yards away.

Thankfully, before Gateshead our day had started at Heaton, where I should have photographed No 26500, the antique electric still in service, especially since it had been built at Brush just up the road from Leicester, but I didn't, instead picking on one of the 'A3s' and managing to capture a telegraph post right through the middle of its tender, rendering the picture unusable.

Twenty-three of the Raven 'Q6' 0-8-0s filled Blaydon shed (52C), together with 12 'K1' 2-6-0s, but by now there was only one thought in our heads – a return visit to Carlisle.

The boys all agreed that our visit to Carlisle certainly didn't disappoint, especially after seeing six 'Clan' Pacifics, which, with the addition of our recent visitor in Leicester, left only three of the class not observed. Three Scottish 'Duchesses' – *Buccleuch*, *Atholl* and *Montrose* – also added to the magic, together with some 'Princesses', including one *Margaret Rose* in steam – a real bonus considering the withdrawal of the other class members a few months before. Canal shed once again delivered some Scottish 'Pacifics', and it was nice to still see a couple of smaller engines from North of the Border, ancient Caledonian 0-6-0s, at Kingmoor.

No 72005 *Clan Macgregor* at Carlisle Kingmoor.

Carlisle Kingmoor (12A)

Class	Number/Name
Diesel shunters	D2083, D4009
BR Type 4	D91, D94, D108, D138
2-6-4T Class 4	42233, 42320
2-6-0 5MT	42757, 42830, 42832, 42834, 42857, 42884, 42887, 42899, 42905, 42906, 42911,
2-6-0 Class 2	43027
0-6-0 3F/4F	43622, 43902, 44019, 44181, 44183, 44451
4-6-0 Class 5	44672, 44673, 44674, 44727, 44792, 44877, 44900, 44901, 44903, 44993, 45018, 45082, 45083, 45100, 45120, 45159, 45177, 45245, 45254, 45330, 45334, 45364, 45365, 45466
4-6-0 'Jubilee'	45640 *Frobisher*, 45657 *Tyrwhitt*, 45697 *Achilles*, 45713 *Renown*, 45716 *Swiftsure*, 45718 *Dreadnought*, 45719 *Glorious*, 45728 *Defiance*
4-6-0 'Royal Scot'	46140 *The King's Royal Rifle Corps*
4-6-2 'Princess Royal'	46200 *Princess Royal*, 46203 *Princess Margaret Rose*, 46207 *Princess Arthur of Connaught*
4-6-2 'Princess Coronation'	46230 *Duchess of Buccleuch*, 46231 *Duchess of Atholl*, 46257 *City of Salford*, 46232 *Duchess of Montrose*, 46244 *King George VI*, 46255 *City of Hereford*
0-6-0T 3F	47281, 47332, 47358, 47467, 47471, 47492
2-8-0 8F	48399, 48708
0-6-0 3F	57602, 57653
4-6-0 BR Class 5	73056, 73058

Carlisle Kingmoor (12A) continued	
Class	**Number/Name**
4-6-2 'Britannia'	70019 *Lightning*, 70023 *Venus*, 70050 *Firth of Clyde*
4-6-2 'Clan'	72000 *Clan Buchanan*, 72002 *Clan Campbell*, 72003 *Clan Fraser*, 72005 *Clan Macgregor*, 72007 *Clan Mackintosh*, 72009 *Clan Stewart*
Carlisle Upperby (12B)	
Diesel shunter	D3087
EE Type 4	D376
2-6-4T Class 4	42238, 42337, 42351, 42393
2-6-0 5MT	42947
2-6-0 4MT	43028
0-6-0 4F	44081
4-6-0 Class 5	44765, 44786, 44831, 44892, 45000, 45019, 45025, 45081, 45244, 45281, 45289, 45307, 45317, 45323, 45342, 45347, 45402
4-6-0 'Patriot'	45523 *Bangor*, 45526 *Morecambe and Heysham*, 45545 *Planet*
4-6-0 'Jubilee'	45588 *Kashmir*, 45613 *Kenya*, 45691 *Orion*, 45721 *Impregnable*, 45732 *Sanspareil*, 45738 *Samson*, 45742 *Connaught*
4-6-2 'Princess Coronation'	46220 *Coronation*, 46236 *City of Bradford*, 46246 *City of Manchester*, 46252 *City of Leicester*
2-6-0 Class 2	46434, 46455, 46458
0-6-0T 3F	47265, 47377, 47408, 47562, 47602, 47614
2-8-0 8F	48722

Carlisle Canal (12C)	
Diesel shunters	12084, 12085, 12086
BRC&W Type 2	D5317
2-6-4T Class 4	42067, 42081, 42095, 42440
2-6-0 5MT	42720
2-6-0 4MT	43045, 43139
4-6-2 'A3'	60057 Ormonde, 60068 Sir Visto
4-6-2 'A1'	60159 Bonnie Dundee, 60162 Saint Johnstoun
4-6-2 'A2'	60536 Trimbush
2-6-2 'V2'	60843, 60951, 60959, 60969, 60971, 60980
4-6-0 'B1'	61064, 61239, 61341, 61357, 61359, 61395
0-6-0 'J39'	64877, 64888, 64895, 64899
0-6-0 'J36'	65237, 65293, 65321
0-6-2T 'N15'	69155

Our journey home that Sunday followed the West Coast route, and was to be a bit of an anti-climax. We visited four more sheds, Tebay (12H), where 'Jubilee' No 45686 *St Vincent* passed by, followed by Carnforth (24L), where five other members of that class were present together with the former 'Condor' express freight diesels Nos D5706 and D5708, now exiled to the North West. Continuing south we visited Lancaster (24J), where two unrebuilt 'Patriots', Nos 45505 *The Royal Army Ordnance Corps* and 45507 *Royal Tank Corps*, were observed, before our last shed at Lostock Hall (24C).

All in all it was a wonderful trip, which saw me record a huge total of 770 locomotives 'copped'. Looking back at our weekend travels I now wonder just what frame of mind I was in when I returned to school the following Monday morning – probably in a world of my own full of trains. But of course we were young with little responsibility to handle and full of energy, and despite only a few months left at school I spent very little time thinking about the future other than where our next outing would be.

As it turned out, May proved to be a bumper month for us spotters, with the Great Central Club organising visits to Sheffield and Doncaster, including the latter's great railway works, as well as a return to London and the opportunity to go around one of the capital's largest sheds, Stratford (30A).

Locally 'Britannias' continued to dominate the scene, with Immingham 'Pacifics' on the 'Fish' being turned out in an excellent condition, a credit to their shed cleaning staff in a day and age when manpower shortages on the railways were common. Sadly, things were to worsen even more in the next few years, reflected by further deterioration in the external appearance of a lot of express steam locomotives, and also their maintenance. Despite the number of sheds we enjoyed visiting, a lot of others were now less appealing to this spotter; a good guide to this was the depot's shed code, where usually the most exciting facility carried an 'A' suffix, for example 36A, Doncaster. The Sheffield area sheds were a good example of what I'm talking about, with few that I would describe as exciting, because the majority were full of freight engines. For me, on the day it was all about getting to Doncaster, its works and shed, and the chance of seeing some of the East Coast's famous 'Pacifics'.

Langworth Junction (41J), our first stop on the GC Club's trip, was a prime example, filled with no fewer than 28 'O4' 2-8-0s together with 16 'Austerity' engines. The two sheds at Staveley followed, including the roundhouse at Barrow Hill, where three 'Jubilees' and 'Royal Scot' No 46164 *The Artist's Rifleman* were on shed, together with a couple of ancient Johnson 0-6-0s, Nos 41739 and 41763, which had lived there forever. One thing I've always remembered about going around this depot was a particular odour in the air, which I think came from the nearby foundry or works, though at the time Big Stu insisted it was Stan who was responsible. A return visit to Sheffield Darnall (41A) saw no sign of the ex-GCR 'Directors' that we had seen on our last visit,

Leicester Great Central, May 1962	
Date	**Number/Name**
Wednesday 2 May	4-6-0 'Jubilee' 45695 *Minotaur*
	4-6-0 'B1' 61068
	4-6-2 'Britannia' 70039 *Sir Christopher Wren*
Friday 4 May	4-6-2 'Britannia' 70039 *Sir Christopher Wren*
Friday 11 May	4-6-2 'Britannia' 70039 *Sir Christopher Wren*
	4-6-0 'B1' 61116
	2-6-0 'K3' 61883
Monday 14 May	4-6-2 'Britannia' 70037 *Hereward the Wake*
	2-6-0 'K3' 61906
Friday 18 May	4-6-2 'Britannia' 70041 *Sir John Moore*
	4-6-0 'B1' 61018 *Gnu*
Tuesday 22 May	4-6-2 'Britannia' 70035 *Rudyard Kipling*
	2-6-0 'K3' 61872
Friday 25 May	4-6-2 'Britannia' 70035 *Rudyard Kipling*
	4-6-0 'B16' 61437
Monday 28 May	2-6-0 'K3' 61895, 61807
Leicester Midland	
Saturday 26 May	4-6-0 'Patriot' 45522 *Prestatyn*
	2-6-4T Class 4 42338
	2-8-0 8F 48349 (2E, Northampton)

but despite the shed now being under London Midland Region control we were still able to observe a large number of Eastern 4-6-0 'B1s', including a couple of named ones, Nos 61027 *Madoqua* and 61033 *Dibatag*. The next two sheds, Canklow (41D) and Mexborough (41F) contained no fewer than 47 more 'Austerity' locomotives, so the least said the better.

Finally we reached Doncaster and its works, known as the 'Plant', where we found electric locomotives for the West Coast Main Line under construction, together with seven 'A4s' under repair, including Haymarket's No 60011 *Empire of India*, which I 'copped', as well as a couple of rare Scottish 'A2s', Nos 60528 *Tudor Minstrel* and 60530 *Sayajirao*.

Following Doncaster we visited Frodingham (36C), both Retford sheds, and Colwick (40E), all of which being freight depots were once again full of Eastern Region 2-8-0 and 'Austerity' locos, quite a number of which I hadn't seen before, helping me underline 286 'cops' for the day in my *abc* 'Combine'.

Doncaster Works, 13 May 1962	
Class	**Number/Name**
2-6-2 'V2'	60950
4-6-2 'A4'	60003 *Andrew K. McCosh*, 60007 *Sir Nigel Gresley*, 60008 *Dwight D. Eisenhower*, 60011 *Empire of India*, 60015 *Quicksilver*, 60025 *Falcon*, 60027 *Merlin*
4-6-2 'A3'	60037 *Hyperion*, 60054 *Prince of Wales*, 60061 *Pretty Polly*, 60093 *Coronach*, 60105 *Victor Wild*, 60106 *Flying Fox*
4-6-2 'A1'	60115 *Meg Merrilies*, 60116 *Hal o' the Wynd*, 60123 *H. A. Ivatt*, 60140 *Balmoral*, 60146 *Peregrine*, 60148 *Aboyeur*
4-6-2 'A2'	60522 *Straight Deal*
4-6-0 'B1'	61000 *Springbok*, 61059, 61089, 61109
2-6-0 'K3'	61822, 61922 (both withdrawn)

No 60037 *Hyperion*, ex-works at Doncaster. *Leslie Freeman/transporttreasuary.co.uk*

Doncaster Works continued	
Class	**Number/Name**
2-6-0 'K1'	62034, 62036, 62039, 62054
2-8-0 'O2'/'O4'	63646, 63663, 63796, 63942, 63943, 63955
0-6-0T 'J50'	68911, 68917, 68961 (works shunters)
4-6-2 'Britannia'	70011 *Hotspur*, 70040 *Clive of India*
4-6-0 BR Class 5	73015
Diesel shunters	D2409, D3442, D3450, D3484, D4064
EE Type 4	D390
BRC&W Type 2	D5386, D5387
Brush Type 2	D5647, D5649, D5670, D5806, D5835, D5840
EE Type 3	D6714, D6737, D6738
EE Type 1	D8022, D8059
BTH Type 1	D8200, D8217, D8219
EE Type 5	D9008
AL5 (new-build electrics)	E3074/75/76/77/78/79/80/81/82/83/84/85

Around this time I think I must have made my first tentative step to finding employment. Of course, getting a job in the early 1960s, unlike today, was not difficult; the then big manufacturing businesses in Leicester, particularly the hosiery and shoe industries, were looking to recruit secondary school leavers. Looking back, these were confusing times for me, especially when considering what sort of job I was going to try and find, because I didn't have a clue other than I didn't want to follow my father into the building trade, especially as I was rubbish at woodwork despite Dad being a carpenter. I do remember our school organising just one career evening for us Year 4s, which was attended by British Railways, among others, and I did have a chat with the representative, who

Doncaster (36A)	
Class	**Number/Name**
4-6-2 'A3'	60059 *Tracery*, 60075 *St Frusquin* (passed by), 60100 *Spearmint*, 60107 *Royal Lancer*
4-6-2 'A1'	60113 *Great Northern*, 60121 *Curlew*, 60125 *Scottish Union*, 60128 *Bongrace*, 60139 *Sea Eagle*, 60144 *King's Courier*, 60149 *Amadis*
4-6-2 'A2'	60520 *Owen Tudor*, 60523 *Sun Castle*, 60533 *Happy Knight*
2-6-2 'V2'	60803, 60839, 60841, 60878, 60896, 60908, 60912, 60921, 60930, 60935, 60943, 60966
4-6-0 'B1'	61001 *Springbok*, 61003 *Gazelle*, 61036 *Ralph Assheton*, 61055, 61122, 61127, 61128, 61135, 61145, 61156, 61157, 61170, 61196, 61214, 61250 *A. Harold Bibby*, 61251 *Oliver Bury*, 61255 61314 61316 61360
2-6-0 'K2'	61742 (withdrawn)
2-6-0 'K3'	61834, 61896, 61919 (all withdrawn), 61895
2-6-0 'K1'	62020, 62036, 62038, 62053, 62068, 62069
2-8-0 'O2'/'O4'	63593, 63618, 63704, 63718, 63736, 63738, 63759, 63802, 63858, 63887, 63935, 63951, 63962, 63968, 63981, 63985, 63986
0-6-0 'J6'	64253 (withdrawn)
0-6-0T 'J50'	68928, 68972
4-6-2 'Britannia'	70009 *Alfred the Great*, 70053 *Moray Firth*
4-6-0 BR Class 5	73165

Doncaster (36A) continued	
Class	**Number/Name**
2-6-0 BR Class 2	78022, 78023, 78024, 78025
2-8-0 'WD'	90003, 90008, 90035, 90042, 90130, 90144, 90166, 90208, 90223, 90224, 90225, 90255, 90269, 90270, 90286, 90293, 90296, 90395, 90447, 90476, 90490, 90496, 90501, 90551, 90560, 90627, 90636, 90732 *Vulcan*
9-10-0 BR 9F	92168, 92171, 92172, 92174, 92179, 92189, 92191, 92192, 92195, 92200
Diesel shunters	D2401, D3439, D3153, D3621
Brush Type 2	D5839
EE Type 4	D270, D275, D386
EE Type 5	D9021, D9018 (passed by)

completely put me off, as I seemed to know more about railways than he did.

In between our trips in May, our Club organised a survey of the Midland main line rail traffic passing through Leicester on a Saturday. This was conducted by

A British Railways recruitment poster aimed at us school leavers, with only engine cleaners and apprentice jobs being offered in the motive power area.

134

small groups of members stationed at various vantage points in and around the city, with yours truly, Stan and Big Stu stationed just south of London Road station. We arrived at our post close to the Cattle Market Sidings just off Welford Road around 9.00am with instructions to record all passing rail traffic, the engines involved, and the various passenger trains they hauled, helped hopefully by the destination boards carried on the carriages. Despite it being the middle of May, I remember it being a dull damp day, and as we were in the open without cover thankfully the rain held off and we stayed until around 4.00pm, after which our observations concluded with a trip to the 'Birdcage' where 'Britannia' No 70003 *John Bunyan* from 31B, March shed, was noted. I think it's fair to say our survey was very basic, but looking at the express trains recorded it did confirm how diesel power had ousted steam from most of the Midlands passenger traffic. I do remember, however, how nice it was to see another

Great Central Railway Society, Leicester (Midland) survey, Saturday 19 May	
Locomotive	**Train**
D130	Manchester-London
D110	Sheffield-London
75058	Local
44013	Empty stock
46403	Local
D89	London-Manchester
D5383 & D5385	London-Nottingham
44247	Light engine
48018	Freight
45274	Freight
D65	London-Manchester
D128	London-Leicester

Locomotive	Train
45407	Special passenger
D78	'Thames-Clyde Express'
45267	Special passenger
45624 *St Helena*	Freight
45034	Special passenger
43017	Local train
46115 *Scots Guardsman*	Manchester-London
D126	Light engine
70044 *Earl Haig*	Bradford-London
45416	Special train
D93	London-Leicester
D13	Leicester-London
45059	Special passenger
D164	London-Nottingham
D331	London-Manchester
D131	London-Manchester

'Britannia', *Earl Haig*, appear during the afternoon, as she was a Leeds Holbeck engine at the time, and I think quite rare through Leicester. Our observations, together with those from the rest of the lads, were handed in at the next Great Central Society meeting, after which I can't remember anything being produced, but luckily I kept a record of the day; note that DMUs are, again, not mentioned.

So on to London the following weekend, and a return to the capital, not only with Stratford (30A) on the agenda, but also hopefully an opportunity at last to see a large number of the Southern Region's steam engines, whose various classes had proven to be the most elusive for this Midlands-based trainspotter, having concluded that the chances of seeing one of them working into our area on a regular freight or passenger service was nil. Up to 1962 I can't remember hearing of a Southern locomotive ever being seen on shed locally. Looking back, it felt that an 'Iron Curtain' seemed to surround Southern steam locomotives, preventing their passage north into the East Midlands, but I'm pleased to report the curtain was eventually pierced on a couple of occasions in 1963 – but more about that later. It's true that I had observed such engines before and was very excited with the prospect of visiting three of the Southern's main depots and seeing some of its 'top link' locomotives, especially the famous Bulleid 'Pacifics'. One that I was to observe later that day at Nine Elms proved particularly significant; 'Battle of Britain' No 34054 *Lord Beaverbrook* was, according to my records, the 10,000th railway engine number I had collected since starting my hobby. I should add, before we actually move on to the trip itself, that I'm now a proud owner of a Hornby Railways OO-gauge model of *Lord Beaverbrook*, which sits proudly in my model engine display case at home, thus providing a great reminder of her place in my trainspotting adventures all those years ago.

I collected 301 'cops' on this trip, with 101 of them at one shed alone, Stratford, of which only 37 were steam locomotives. Old Oak Common accounted for another 42, with the three Southern sheds adding another 81 engines to my collection from that region, 18 of which were Bulleid 'Pacifics'. New diesels were also evident, with No 10001 being observed at Bletchley, where it had been working on local passenger workings into Euston, and No 10202 at Willesden. The trip also provided me with my first sightings of both the new 'Hymek' and 'Western' classes of diesel-hydraulics, which were noted at Old Oak together with the prototype Type 4 locomotive No D0260 *Lion*, which had just returned to service having failed at Leamington after its main generator had flashed over on 17 May. *Lion* certainly looked different, painted white with five gold stripes along the bottom half of its bodyside, a quite daring livery when considering the railway environment in which she was operating, and one

No 34054 *Lord Beaverbrook* in April 1962. *Ron Smith/transporttreasuary.co.uk*

wonders how they ever managed to keep it clean. Unfortunately, her makers, the Birmingham Railway Carriage & Wagon Company, failed to win the large order for Type 4 diesels, which went to Brush Traction for what later became its Class 47s, and she was withdrawn a year later and scrapped.

On the steam front, despite withdrawals it was nice to see three of the 'King' Class engines at Old Oak, and on the Southern a couple of the famous 'School' Class locomotives as well as a single 'Lord Nelson' at Nine Elms, where I also came across five BR Standard Class 5 4-6-0s allocated to the Southern Region and now carrying names associated with the 'King Arthur' legend.

I was also obviously pleased to see the 'Bulleids', especially the unrebuilt version of the 'West Country' and 'Battle of Britain' classes, which looked so different from other express locomotives, thanks to their unique engine 'air-smoothed' casing and the designer's lighter yet more filled-in wheels. One engine also worth mentioning was 'Black 5' No 44962 in immaculate condition on shed at Willesden, having recently been on a Royal Train duty, with sister engine No 44942, conveying the Queen to Coventry for the consecration of the new cathedral.

At the time I wasn't to know it, but our visit to Neasden (14D) proved to be the last as it closed a few weeks afterwards at the start of the 1962 BR Summer Timetable in June. Perhaps

London, Sunday 27 May 1962

Bletchley (1E)

Class	Number/Name
2-6-2T Class 4	42105, 42106, 42454, 42579, 42586, 42615
2-6-0 5MT	42772, 42854
4-6-0 Class 5	44716, 45044, 45089, 45292, 45393
0-6-0T 3F	47348, 47521
2-8-0 8F	48203, 48343, 48427, 48490, 48549, 48646, 48668
0-8-0 7F	49094
4-6-0 BR Class 4	75013, 75028, 75038, 75039, 75059
2-6-2T Br Class 2	84002
BR Co-Co 5P/5F	10001
BR Type 2	D5011, D5015, D5020, D5033, D5037, D5144

Cricklewood (14A)

Class	Number/Name
2-6-2T Class 4	42283, 42329, 42336, 42686
2-6-0 4MT	43031, 43118, 43120, 43121
0-6-0 3F/4F	43428, 43947, 44259, 44297
4-6-0 Class 5	44912
0-6-0T 3F	47211, 47248, 47432, 47435, 47453, 47462, 47543
2-8-0 8F	48141, 48142, 48304, 48313, 48324, 48367, 48378, 48441, 48517 48678
4-6-0 BR Class 5	73045
2-10-0 BR 9F	92021, 92083, 92160
Diesel shunters	D12085 D3022 D3305
BR Type 4	D102

Cricklewood (14A) continued	
Class	**Number/Name**
BR Type 2	D5084, D5085, D5086, D5091, D5092, D5093

Kentish Town (14B)	
2-6-2T Class 3	40022, 40026, 40100, 40111, 40203
2-6-2T Class 4	42227, 42156, 42334, 42335 42610, 42685
0-6-0 4F	44235, 44532, 44572
4-6-0 Class 5	44840, 44872, 44920, 44985, 45267
4-6-0 'Jubilee'	45605 *Cyprus*, 45628 *Somaliland*
0-6-0T 3F	47202, 47223, 47261, 47402, 47442, 47449, 47502, 47554, 47611/45
2-10-0 BR 9F	92028
BRC&W Type 2	D5383, D5384, D5386, D5387, D5388
BR Type 4	D58, D139

Devon Road (Bow) (1D)	
Diesel shunters	D2901, D2903, D2904, D2905, D2906, D2907
EE Type 1	D8008, D8012, D8013, D8014, D8016, D8017, D8040, D8041

Stratford (30A)	
Class	**Number/Name**
4-6-0 'B1'	61149, 61253, 61283, 61311, 61326, 61329, 61335, 61362, 61375/78
4-6-0 'B12'	61572 (preserved)
0-6-0 'J19'	64657, 64664, 64673
0-6-0 'J15'	65361, 65445, 65460, 65462, 65464, 65465, 65476
0-6-0 'J17'	65581, 65586

2-6-4T 'L1'	67703, 67715, 67716, 67723, 67724, 67729, 67730, 67731, 67734 67735, 67737
0-6-0T (Dept'l loco)	32 (68370)
0-6-0T 'J67'/'J69'	68499, 68542, 68556, 68565, 68566, 68600, 68621, 68626, 68635
0-6-2T 'N7'	69621, 69632, 69640, 69646, 69671, 69692, 69697, 69725
2-6-4T BR Class 4	80097
2-8-0 'WD'	90034
EE Type 4	D204, D206
BR Type 2	D5050, D5068
0-4-0 shunters	D2956, D2958
0-6-0 shunters	D12111, D12128, D12130, D2216, D2222, D2226, D2228, D3303, D3500, D3609, D3637, D3682, D3683
Brush Type 2	D5503, D5506, D5509, D5511, D5512, D5517, D5529, D5576, D5577, D5578, D5581, D5585, D5586, D5587, D5589, D5591, D5592, D5593, D5594, D5596, D5597, D5622, D5627, D5632, D5633, D5634, D5635, D5637, D5638, D5660, D5694, D5695, D5800
EE Type 2	D5902, D5903, D5904, D5906, D5909
EE Type 3	D6702, D6705, D6709, D6717, D6718, D6726
BTH Type 1	D8224, D8225, D8227, D8228, D8229, D8230, D8231, D8232, 8233/36
NB Type 1	D8400, D8401, D8402, D8403, D8405, D8406, D8407, D8408, D8409
Plaistow (33A) *(officially closed)*	
0-6-2T 3F	41981 (last in class)

Plaistow (33A) *(officially closed)* continued	
Class	**Number/Name**
2-6-2T Class 4	42219, 42221, 42223, 42254, 42255, 42257, 42278, 42282, 42519, 42520, 42529, 42684
0-6-0T 3F	47328, 47331, 47355
2-6-4T BR Class 4	80070, 80073, 80076, 80078, 80096, 80099, 80103, 80105, 80131, 80133
2-8-0 'WD'	90023, 90093, 90196, 90244, 90256
Nine Elms (70A)	
0-4-4T 'M7'	30039, 30057, 30249, 30321
4-6-0 'Lord Nelson'	30860 *Lord Hawke*
4-4-0 'Schools'	30912 *Downside*
2-6-0 'N'/'N1'	31816, 31821
2-6-0 'U'/'U1'	31617, 31621, 31624, 31626, 31634, 31636, 31796
0-6-2T 'E4'	32472, 32473, 32487, 32557
0-6-0 'Q1'	33006, 33017, 33018
4-6-2 'West Country'	34006 *Bude*, 34018 *Axminster*, 34021 *Dartmoor*, 34099 *Lynmouth*, 34108 *Wincanton*
4-6-2 'Battle of Britain'	34054 *Lord Beaverbrook* (10,000th engine recorded), 34070 *Manston*, 34077 *603 Squadron*, 34086 *219 Squadron*, 34087 *145 Squadron*
4-6-2 'Merchant Navy'	35001 *Channel Packet*, 35008 *Orient Line*, 35016 *Elders Fyffes*, 35017 *Belgian Marine*, 35024 *East Asiatic Line* 35029 *Ellerman Lines*
4-6-0 BR Class 5	73082 *Camelot*, 73085 *Melisande*, 73088 *Joyous Gard*, 73115 *King Pellinore*, 73118 *King Leodegrance*

No 34018 *Axminster* at Nine Elms. *A. Swain/transporttreasuary.co.uk*

4-6-0 BR Class 4	75079
0-6-0PT '5700'	3633, 4634, 4672, 4681, 4692, 4698
Diesel shunters	15211, D3271, D3461
Stewarts Lane (73A)	
0-6-0PT '5700'	4631
Diesel shunters	D15229, D2284 D3222 D3321
BRC&W Type 3	D6554, D6560, D6581
BR Class CC (electric)	20001
BR Bo-Bo (electric)	E5001, E5005, E5006, E5008, E5015, E5016, E5018
BR Bo-Bo (electro-diesel)	E6001
4-4-0 'Schools'	30926 *Repton*,
2-6-0 'N'/'N1'	31410, 31411, 31821, 31823, 31824
2-6-0 'U1'	31893, 31896
0-6-0 'C'	31592
4-6-2 'Battle of Britain'	34089 *602 Squadron*
4-6-0 BR Class 4	75074
2-6-4T BR Class 4	80012, 80034

Bricklayers Arms (73B)	
Class	**Number/Name**
Diesel shunters	D2287, D2293, D3462, 15201, 15202, 15212, 15213, 15216, 15221, 15225, 15226, 15227
BR Type 2	D5008
BRC&W Type 3	D6536, D6538, D6548, D6572, D6577, D6578
0-6-0 'Q'	30534
4-4-0 'D1'	31305
0-6-0 'C'	31267, 31510
2-6-0 'N'	31825, 31828, 31829, 31872, 31873
4-6-2 'West Country'	34012 *Launceston*, 34013 *Okehampton*, 34040 *Crewkerne*, 34101 *Hartland*
4-6-2 'Battle of Britain'	34050 *Royal Observer Corps*, 34085 *501 Squadron*, 34088 *213 Squadron*
2-6-4T BR Class 4	80082, 80083, 80084
Old Oak Common (81A)	
4-6-0 'County'	1011 *County of Chester*, 1015 *County of Gloucester*
0-6-0PT '1500'	1504, 1506
2-8-0 '2800'	3816
0-6-0PT '5700'	3646, 3750, 3754, 8756, 8757, 8758, 8759, 8761, 8763, 8768, 8771, 9640, 9658, 9659, 9661, 9700, 9704, 9709, 9758
2-8-0 '4700'	4701, 4704, 4705
4-6-0 'Hall'	5931 *Hatherley Hall*, 5932 *Haydon Hall*, 5939 *Tangley Hall*, 5944 *Ickenham Hall*, 5967 *Bickmarsh Hall*, 6910 *Gossington Hall*, 6920 *Barningham Hall*, 6941 *Fillongley Hall*

No 8759 at Old Oak Shed in 1963. *Ted Reading*

4-6-0 'Modified Hall'	6961 *Stedham Hall*, 6966 *Witchingham Hall*, 7921 *Edstone Hall*
4-6-0 'Castle'	4082 *Windsor Castle*, 5016 *Montgomery Castle*, 5032 *Usk Castle*, 5034 *Corfe Castle*, 5036 *Lyonshall Castle*, 5056 *Earl of Powis*, 5060 *Earl of Berkeley*, 5077 *Fairey Battle*, 5084 *Reading Abbey*, 5085 *Evesham Abbey*, 7004 *Eastnor Castle*, 7010 *Banbury Castle*, 7020 *Gloucester Castle*, 7032 *Hartlebury Castle*

No 7020 *Gloucester Castle* at Old Oak Common in 1962. *Ted Reading*

Class	Number/Name
4-6-0 'King'	6014 *King Henry VII*, 6021 *King Richard II*, 6026 *King John*
2-6-2T '6100'	6125, 6135, 6141, 6142, 6164, 6169
4-6-0 'Grange'	6852 *Headbourne Grange*, 6863 *Dolhywel Grange*, 6864 *Dymock Grange*
0-6-0PT '9400'	8459, 9405, 9407, 9419, 9420
2-10-0 BR 9F	92000, 92204, 92217, 92218
4-6-0 Class 5	44824
2-8-0 8F	48410, 48412
BRC&W Type 4	D0260 *Lion*
NB Type 4 'Warship'	D602 *Bulldog*
BR Type 4 'Warship'	D800 *Sir Brian Robertson*, D817 *Foxhound*, D828 *Magnificent*, D834 *Pathfinder*

Prototype No D0260 *Lion* at Old Oak Common.

BR Type 4 'Western'	D1003 *Western Pioneer*
BR Type 3 'Hymek'	D7031
Diesel shunters	D3032, D3398, D3597, D3962, D4000, D4003

Willesden (1A)

Diesel shunters	D3177, D3834
2-6-2T Class 3	40006, 40080, 40099, 40128, 40144, 40157, 40201
2-6-4T Class 4	42066, 42068, 42101, 42117, 42238, 42350, 42351, 42366, 42470, 42478, 42576, 42611, 42627
2-6-0 5MT	42953
0-6-0 4F	44348, 44442
4-6-0 Class 5	44710, 44714, 44911, 44916, 44962, 45048, 45061, 45130, 45191 45222, 45282, 45331, 45354, 45373, 45418, 45434
4-6-0 'Patriot'	45529 *Stephenson*
4-6-0 'Jubilee'	45582 *Central Provinces*, 45601 *British Guiana*, 45617 *Mauritius*, 45710 *Irresistible*
4-6-0 'Royal Scot'	46111 *Royal Fusilier*, 46147 *The Northamptonshire Regiment*, 46159 *The Royal Air Force*, 46169 *The Boy Scout*
2-6-0 Class 2	46424, 46472
0-6-0T 3F	47302, 47304, 47501
2-8-0 8F	48134, 48171, 48258, 48301, 48368, 48495, 48601, 48604, 48629, 48633, 48637, 48650, 48656, 48723, 48754
0-8-0 7F	49078, 49413
4-6-2 'Britannia'	70004 *William Shakespeare*, 70032 *Tennyson*, 70042 *Lord Roberts*

Willesden (1A) continued	
Class	Number/Name
4-6-0 BR Class 5	73013, 73014
4-6-0 BR Class 4	75030, 75037
2-10-0 BR 9F	92111
EE Type 4	D230 *Scythia*
BR 1Co–Co1	10202
BR Type 2	D5002, D5018, D5023, D5024, D5026, D5027, D5028, D5030, D5073
EE Type 1	D8002, D8004, D8006, D8007, D8018
Neasden (14D)	
2-6-4T Class 4	42070, 42087, 42090, 42178, 42251, 42253, 42279, 42281
4-6-0 Class 5	44688, 44690, 45020, 45111
4-6-0 'Patriot'	45669 *Fisher*
4-6-0 BR Class 5	73010, 73034, 73035, 73066, 73156, 73157
2-6-0 BR Class 4	76036, 76037, 76038, 76039, 76041, 76042

the signs were there, with its allocation reduced by half since our visit a couple of years before, and all trace of its previous Eastern Region connection gone, with none of its locomotives present. Another sign of the changes taking place on the rail network at an ever-increasing pace, and certainly at Stratford, was noting the largest number of diesels I had ever seen at a motive power depot.

Moving away from railways, I should mention that there was one very excited member on this trip, Big Stu, an ardent bus enthusiast, who was over the moon that morning when he discovered that travel to London was on Mr Lester's new coach, a 'Europa', and the driver soon made it very clear we were not to drop any litter on the new vehicle's floor; we were also advised to wipe our feet before entering it after shed visits.

Moving into June 1962 my records show that after all my trainspotting activity in May it was followed by a very quiet month, where apart from local spotting at Leicester only one visit to nearby Nuneaton took place – the reason for this was school exams. Yes, it was time for study and revision as I was taking a number of subjects in the College of Preceptors Certificate Examination that month at school, so reluctantly I had to get my head down, especially as I suffered from nerves and struggled with exams, despite my classwork being acceptable. I knew I was good at the subjects I loved – history, religious education and English, particularly literature – but things I didn't like, and there were an awful lot of them, forget it, so I won't dwell on my academic achievements further.

I remember that, after taking our exams, we sought some light relief to celebrate, which Big Stu insists I should bring to your attention. I was forced to accompany him, Stan, Colin and Doug to the Cameo Picture House in town one evening to see a rather interesting film. We were only 15 and I have to admit I was nervous because the film carried an over-18 certificate, and was therefore not suitable for young impressionable boys like us. Waiting to pay for admission at the box office seemed to take an eternity, but amazingly we all got in, even little Colin, who never looked a teenager, let alone 18. Once inside we bumped into about half our school year sitting there in the dingy picture house, all of us curious regarding

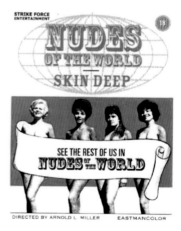

the film's subject, which I admit had nothing to do with trains! Well, my book is about the adventures of a trainspotter, and 50 years ago this proved to be one of them for our gang, whom I remember went on to debate at length both at school, down the Midland, and at the GC Club regarding whether ladies should be better off wearing clothing when playing volleyball. Say no more!

You may remember that I've mentioned before how much Nuneaton figured in our early trainspotting days, with regular visits, and it became our next trip during our school Whitsuntide holidays that June. We travelled by train this time from London Road, and with trainspotting barred from the platforms of Trent Valley station we soon made our way to a recreational ground we had discovered just south of it, quite close to the old Abbey Street station, from where we could watch both the West Coast expresses storming by and also see the Birmingham to Leicester branch-line traffic. We had found the area, which was about a 15-minute walk from the station, in the early days before the electrification wires were installed. I remember there was an old wooden pedestrian footbridge crossing the main line on which we climbed, enabling us to get great views of any expresses as they approached. I'm back there now in 1960, watching a maroon 'Coronation' 'Pacific' approaching at speed proudly displaying its 'Royal Scot' headboard, then roaring under the bridge with us boys cheering at seeing the all-important name plate and of course engine number as she thunders by – believe me it was magical! You can see from the list of trains that I did try to identify the expresses we saw, using information from the destination boards displayed on the sides of the coaches.

We also managed to sneak around Nuneaton shed successfully, but out of a healthy 48 engines present I only managed to 'cop' three of her allocation, 2-6-0 No 43115, 3F 0-6-0 No 43607 and 'Jinty' No 47294. Talking about going round 2B reminds me of an occasion on an earlier trip when on the way to the shed, climbing over the steel boundary fence, I managed to rip one of my trouser legs from top to bottom on a spike. Luckily I'd arrived by train and wasn't cycling, and managed to buy some safety pins from a local shop to patch me up for the rest of the day. Of course, it was

Nuneaton, Monday 11 June 1962 (Whitsuntide holidays)	
Leicester - Nuneaton	
Locomotive	**Train**
4-6-0 Class 5 45278	Passed on journey from Leicester to Nuneaton
4-6-0 Class 5 44804	
Nuneaton	
EE Type 4 D300	Manchester-London
EE Type 4 D378	Liverpool-London
EE Type 4 D382	'Royal Scot'
EE Type 4 D289	London-Manchester
EE Type 4 D379	Blackpool-London
EE Type 4 D221 & D222	'Comet'
EE Type 4 D338	'Mancunian'
4-6-2 'Princess Coronation' 46252 *City of Leicester*	London-Perth
EE Type 4 D314	'Emerald Isle'
EE Type 4 D340	'Manxman'

No 46208 *Princess Helena Victoria* with the diverted down 'Ulster Express' at Leamington Spa (Avenue) on 9 June 1962. *R. J. Blenkinsop*

Locomotive	Train
EE Type 4 D317	'Merseyside'
EE Type 4 D298	Unidentified passenger train
4-6-0 BR Class 5 73137	Special
EE Type 4 D287	London-Carlisle
EE Type 4 D315	Unidentified passenger train
EE Type 4 D326	London-Blackpool
4-6-2 'Princess Coronation' 46228 *Duchess of Rutland*	Special
EE Type 4 D235	London-Manchester
EE Type 4 D297	London-Blackpool
EE Type 4 D293	London-Carlisle
EE Type 4 D324	Special
4-6-0 'Jubilee' 45736 *Phoenix*	Special
EE Type 4 D369	Unidentified passenger train
EE Type 4 D372	Unidentified passenger train
4-6-2 'Princess Coronation' 46237 *City of Bristol*	Blackpool-London
EE Type 4 D308	'Royal Scot'
4-6-2 'Princess 'Princess Royal' 46208 *Princess Helena Victoria*	Special
EE Type 4 D343	Special
4-6-2 'Britannia' 70016 *Ariel*	Unidentified passenger train
EE Type 4 D331	Manchester-London
EE Type 4 D255	Light engine

No 71000 *Duke of Gloucester* on the 'Ulster Express' on 9 June.
R. J. Blenkinsop

EE Type 4 D216 *Campania*	Unidentified passenger train
4-6-2 'Princess Coronation' 46237 *City of Bristol*	Special
4-6-0 Class 5 45130	Unidentified passenger train
BR Type 4 D149	Unidentified passenger train
EE Type 4 D377	London-Liverpool
4-6-0 'Jubilee' 45629 *Straits Settlement*	Special

The trainspotting park in Nuneaton is recorded here during one of our biking visits, although I'm not with my usual pals – it's Keith Mapley from the GC Club sliding down the slide with a couple of lads whose names I sadly now can't remember. At least you can see one of the activities we kept ourselves amused with when waiting for trains.

Locomotive	Train
4-6-0 'Royal Scot' 46110 *Grenadier Guardsman*	Liverpool-London
4-6-0 'Royal Scot' 46115 *Scots Guardsman*	Special
EE Type 4 D289	Unidentified passenger train
EE Type 4 D220 *Franconia*	London-Manchester
EE Type 4 D339	London-Blackpool
EE Type 4 D316	Unidentified passenger train
4-6-2 BR Class 8P 71000 *Duke of Gloucester*	Special
EE Type 4 D306	'Shamrock'
EE Type 4 D305	'Mid-Day Scot'

all worth it when I later 'copped' No 46222 *Queen Mary*, a rare Polmadie engine, passing through.

Our Nuneaton visit proved a disappointing day for us steam lovers, with only a few express steam locomotives at work in between the Type 4 diesels, which had now taken over most of the West Coast Main Line's expresses haulage. I was also disappointed not to see any of Nuneaton's allocated 'Patriots', whose non-appearance was explained in the following month's *Modern Railways* magazine, which reported that three of them, Nos 45537, 45541 and 45548, had been withdrawn during the week before our visit, leaving just No 45538 to soldier on until a couple of months later, when it suffered a similar fate. Yes, steam was certainly on the retreat, and perhaps for the first time I felt disillusioned with my hobby, a feeling not helped a couple of weeks later when the full Liverpool to Crewe electric service was introduced, eliminating even more of my steam heroes.

Around this time we were cheered up a bit when a couple

of 'Royal Scots' were transferred to Leicester Central shed, including No 46106 *Gordon Highlander*. They only stayed a couple of weeks, but it was the start of a period when a number of the class did find work on the line towards the end of their working lives. Rounding off my spotting in June, I did manage to 'cop' two steam engines down the Midland with a visit to the 'Birdcage' on Saturday the 9th – Carlisle loco No 44726 and Fowler tank No 42333 – but with no joy there apart from diesels for the rest of the month. I also recorded a couple of 'Jubilees' on shed, No 45669 *Fisher* on the 14th and No 45698 *Mars* on the 21st. Perhaps the most interesting visitor I managed to observe was Great Western 'Hall' Class 4-6-0 No 4970 *Sketty Hall*, which had just been turned on the turntable adjacent to the Central station as I arrived at teatime on the 21st.

Away from railways in July, I started my last month at New Parks Boys School and, although I hadn't a clue what I wanted to do, the focus was now on getting a job. My parents, bless them, had suggested that I consider furthering my education by going to a college, but I was 15 and although still doing my paper round the opportunity to earn a weekly wage looked far more attractive to me. I'm pretty sure that it was our metalwork teacher Mr Denny who made the announcement when we were in class one morning that the British United Shoe Machinery Company, a large engineering business in the city, was looking to recruit school-leavers, subject to an IQ test being taken at the company's premises, and I was invited with a few other boys to go along. To be honest, I had no idea what to expect, but went along to the Union Works, the company's large factory site off Belgrave Road in Leicester, one afternoon and took the test. I vaguely remember it had something to do with shapes and lines that were missing – anyway, I did my best, not having a clue if I was right or wrong. A couple of weeks later a letter dropped through the letterbox at home informing me that I had been offered one of the work places for school-leavers, and I was thrilled to think I had a job and quickly accepted the offer. The company, known locally as the 'BU', was a large employer in Leicester, manufacturing machinery for the shoe industry, which, together with hosiery, was what the city had become famous for. The strange thing, looking back, was that I didn't like engineering, and to be honest at school I didn't think I was very good at it, so it all seemed a bit strange how things happened. I didn't even have the benefit of my pals joining me, with all of us on the job front going our separate ways. Big Stu went to a local garage, Stanley Lance went to learn to be an electrician, and little Colin Field landed some sort of office job. Anyway, with no idea what engineering work I would be doing, my letter advised me of a starting date in early September 1962 and offered me a wage of £2 14s 8d a week, something in the region of £42 today. I was rich at last!

Now that my future was secured I could look forward to my remaining weeks at school followed by a month or so to acclimatise myself with the idea of full-time work, the implications of which, if I'm honest, were a mystery to me as I didn't know what to expect, having had no job experience at all except for my evening paper round. As on the railways, everything was changing for ever, even for me.

My spotting records for July 1962 started with a visit to the Midland on Saturday the 7th where, apart from 'Peak' D124, which I 'copped', I was pleased to note a number of express steam engines for a change, including former Western Region 'Britannia' No 70028 *Royal Star*, three 'Jubilees' and 'Royal Scot' No 46158 *The Loyal Regiment*. Two days later Big Stu and I joined an official visit to our home shed itself, Leicester Midland (15C), which had been organised by the GC Railway Club. This was a special occasion for us, having sneaked around regularly during the previous three years; this was the only time we actually visited it with an official permit. The visit took place in the early evening, following which we cycled down the canal to the Central shed and recorded two 'B1s', Nos 61187 and 61319, and 'K3' No 61897; we also observed the 'Fish' once again, with 'Britannia' No 70035 *Sir Christopher Wren* in charge.

Sadly for me, the total number of locomotives seen for the first time ('cops') at the two sheds was zero. In fact, observing something previously unseen at Leicester, particularly steam, was now becoming a rare event, with the GC line now providing me

Our party at Leicester Midland shed. *Tony Moore*

Leicester Midland (15C) Monday 9 July 1962

Class	Number/Name
2-6-2T Class 2	41228
2-6-4T Class 4	42330, 42331, 42361, 42680
0-6-0 4F	43969, 44034, 44109, 44403, 44414
0-6-0T 3F	47437
4-6-0 Class 5	44811, 44872, 45062
2-8-0 8F	48000, 48089, 48308, 48385, 48628
4-6-2 'Britannia'	70030 *William Wordsworth*
4-6-0 BR Class 5	73159
4-6-0 BR Class 4	75060, 75063
2-10-0 BR 9F	92111
4-6-0 'B1'	61066, 61287
Diesel shunters	D3790, D3791
BR Type 4	D111 (passing by), D82, D113

with the best chance of seeing something new. We were now in our last month at school and, with things winding down, the school organised a Sunday excursion for boys to Windsor and London Airport on the 16th. It proved to be a great day out, visiting the castle in the morning, then in the afternoon visiting the then famous roof gardens at Heathrow, from which you could get a wonderful view of the airport runways. I remember one of the highlights for me was when a jet-powered Caravelle of Air-France came screaming by taking off – it was the first time I had ever seen a jet plane so close up. We were then taken by coaches for a guided tour around the 8-mile airport perimeter, passing the headquarters and workshops of such airlines as BOAC, BEA, TWA, Air-France, Swissair, Pan-American and many more, passing many types of different aircraft ranging from Boeing 707s, Comets and Caravelles to the small propeller aeroplanes such as Dakotas, Vikings and Vanguards, and even the old converted Lancasters renamed Yorks.

So from planes to trains when, after leaving the airport, our coach made its way for an organised tea at Slough, where we were delighted to find that our refreshment stop backed straight onto the busy Great Western main line. Naturally a little trainspotting followed, during which we enjoyed watching the 'Cheltenham Spa Express' pass by hauled by 'Castle' No 7000 *Viscount Portal*, then some diesel power with the Birmingham 'Blue Pullman' and 'Hymek' No D7034 on another named express, the 'Red Dragon', before another 'Castle', No 5024 *Carew Castle*, appeared on a passenger train heading for Paddington.

After our enjoyable outing it was back to school for our last couple of weeks. They say you always remember your teachers, so here's my little tribute to them, even though 50 years have passed. First I loved being in Mr Morris's class – he was a Welsh chap who was our English teacher – then there was Mr Ralph Mason, our maths teacher, who was a lovely man, despite the fact that I struggled with this subject. Religious education was one of my best subjects under Mr Flint, who tarnished his image with me after slapping me across the face for talking in class – quite brutal, but of course those were the days of the cane and the slipper, especially in a boys' school. Incidentally, I'm pleased to report that I avoided both punishments throughout my school years. 'Baby face' Harrison was our art teacher and Mr Eddie Allsop our PE master. Mr Flude took us for science, and Mr Bill Hudson for geography; the latter was a teacher who had played a major role in my school dramatic career, something I've been quite modest about until now, as I appeared in three stage productions over the years: a French nobleman in Shaw's *Joan of Arc*, a deaf widow in *Treasure Island*, and the Bishop of Mid-Wales in a play called *Birds of a Feather*. Needless to say, I was brilliant in all productions and narrowly missed out being selected for a role in a play at Leicester's Little Theatre, failing at the audition stage. I remember that the audition was also attended by a group of young ladies, one of whom was a certain pretty 13-year-old girl named Carolyn, later to become Mrs Warrington, who was successful in being selected for the play, *The Remarkable Mr Pennypacker*. Our paths crossed a few years later, and the rest is history!

There was also Mr Perrott, known by the boys as 'Polly Parrot', who had the impossible task of trying to teach a class of 49 boys French. Sadly I remember that some of the boys made his life hell. Mr Shuttleworth was our history teacher, and Mr Tibbs took us for technical drawing as well as being our final year class master. He was not very tall, with a thin pencil moustache, and there was an aloofness about him – apparently he had held quite a high rank in the Army. Anyway, I always felt scared of him, and didn't enjoy being in his class. Big Stu's memory of him, however, was his threat to keep us in class 20 minutes after our normal finishing time on our very last day of the term as we were about to leave forever, and laughing at us for not realising he was winding us up as we bade farewell to our school days.

Still keen to see Southern steam, our next Great Central Railway Society trip a week later really delivered when we journeyed south to visit a number of the region's sheds as well as the Bluebell Railway, which was now being operated by enthusiasts, with a number of ex-BR locomotives providing the motive power; for the first time our trip was to include a train ride on a preserved railway. Our day started by calling in at Watford shed (1C), where among the 15 steam locos present we came across a couple of old Midland 4-4-0 2P engines, Nos 40657 and 40672, in store. English Electric Type 4 No D378 passed by on the 'Royal Highlander', and 8F No 48120 on a track-laying train. We then moved on to Southall (81C) where, despite my regular visits, I still managed to pick up 11 steam 'cops', including No 5945 *Leckhampton Hall*.

It was into Southern territory after that, with Feltham (70B) our first shed; despite also being familiar because of previous visits, my 11 steam cops just outnumbered the diesel ones, with a large number of Birmingham RC&W Type 3s present. We then went further south to Guildford and its shed (70C), an open roundhouse building that was situated opposite the station close to a tunnel entrance. Here ancient Adams 0-4-0T No 30089 was noted, together with a couple of the famous 'Schools' Class 4-4-0s, Nos 30903 *Charterhouse* and 30906 *Sherborne*. Three Bridges Shed was next, where we found Standard Class 4 tank No 80087 surprisingly in store, then on to the Bluebell Railway, which had been opened as a preserved railway back in August 1960.

Tickets were quickly obtained and our party joined a train hauled by No 55 *Stepney*, a small 'Terrier' tank engine coupled with Adams 'Radial Tank' No 488 for the return journey from Sheffield Park station to Horsted Keynes. A couple of former BR steam locos were also seen: 'Dukedog' 4-4-0 No 9017, which I'd observed on Oswestry Works, and 0-6-0T No 2650, formerly No 58850, which I'd recorded at a Derby Works Open Day.

I can't remember anything about visiting Tunbridge Wells shed (73F), but my record book shows only two class of engines present: five Wainwright Class 'H' 0-4-4T tank engines and ten 2-6-4T BR Standard Class 4s. Nor can I remember the next shed visited, Tonbridge (73J), where ten D6500 diesels outnumbered the steam engines. It was only when we reached Norwood Junction that my spirits were raised after 'copping' all but five of the locomotives present.

Norwood Junction (75C), Sunday 22 July 1962	
Class	**Number/Name**
0-6-0 'Q'	30538
2-6-0 'N'/'N1'	31402, 31828, 31864, 31880
2-6-0 'U1'	31800, 31900, 31903, 31904, 31905, 31906, 31097, 31098, 31910
2-6-4T 'W'	31914, 31917, 31918, 31921, 31915, 31925
2-6-0 'K'	32352
4-6-2 'West Country'	34014 *Budleigh Salterton*
Diesel shunters	D2278, 15203, 15215, D3272, D3459, D3460, D3468, D3469, D4103

Despite having only visited them a couple of months before it was great to return to the London sheds at Nine Elms and Stewarts Lane for the day's last visits. 70A was full of Bulleid 'Pacifics' again, and I was delighted to 'cop' 'Merchant Navy' No 35013 *Blue Funnel* and a couple of the 'West County' Class, Nos 34009 *Lyme Regis* and 34048 *Crediton*. It was also nice to find 'Schools' No 30912 *Downside* on shed again, this time with three other members of the class, two of which, Nos 30934 and 30937, I'd not seen before. Looking at my records I gained 166 'cops' from the 11 sheds visited, leaving the Southern Region section in my Ian Allan *abc* looking a lot healthier after I had finished my underlining session when back home.

Sadly a few weeks later a chain of events took place that led to the Southern trip becoming my last outing with the Great Central Railway Society. Unknown to me, a disagreement had developed within the society's management committee, which was brought to a head at a very fractious AGM when two of its members, Keith Mapley and Graham Holt, refused to serve any further. Both had become quite close friends of mine over the years, and subsequently left the club. I was disappointed with what had occurred and kept in contact with them, and was surprised when they approached me to see if I would be interested in starting up a new railway enthusiasts' club with them.

On learning of their plans, I was excited by their proposals, and also for the opportunity to develop my hobby in a different direction, so readily agreed to join them and help. When rumours started to circulate about the possibility of a new club starting in Leicester, a number of the local spotters appeared interested in joining, which led us to call a meeting in late August at a school hall on Shaftesbury Street. The subsequent turnout proved very encouraging, and included many of my old friends, including Big Stu, Stan and Colin Field, and it was agreed to form a new club, the Midland Railway Society of Leicester. Keith was appointed Chairman at the meeting, and Graham the Secretary. I and three others were elected onto the a new management committee, after which we all soon got down to work quickly agreeing to arrange regular meetings and introduce a membership administration; we also started to plan a programme of shed visits for the rest of the year, which we hoped would attract more members to join – after all, we were now in competition with our old club.

Looking at my record book for the rest of July 1962 and into early August it clearly indicates how trainspotting had taken over my life. I was lucky to be able to allow it do so, as some of my pals didn't have the luxury of time between leaving school and starting work; poor old Big Stu left school on the Friday and started his new working life the following Monday, so I was very lucky.

On the Midland I made a number of observations, spending most of the day at London Road on Saturday the 28th, where I observed three 'Britannias', Nos 70004 *William Shakespeare*, 70006 *Robert Burns* and 70016 *Ariel*, as well as a similar number of 'Jubilees', including No 45685 *Barfleur*, which I recorded on a London to Leeds service. There were diesels about, of course, but I ignored them and added a couple more sightings of 'Royal Scots' Nos 46143 *The South Staffordshire Regiment* and 46164 *The Artist's Rifleman* to my notebook.

One of the interesting workings through the station at the time was an unusual non-stop express from Manchester to

Great Central line, July/August 1962	
Day	**Number/Name**
Monday 23 July	4-6-0 'B1' 61209, 61315
	2-6-0 'K3' 61939
Tuesday 24 July	4-6-0 'B1' 61162
	2-6-0 'K3' 61865, 61939
Wednesday 25 July	2-6-0 'K3' 61889, 61906
	EE Type 3 D6746
Thursday 26 July	4-6-0 'B1' 61337
	2-6-0 'K3' 61871, 61889
	4-6-2 'Britannia' 70014 *Iron Duke*
	4-6-0 'B1' 61319
Monday 30 July	2-6-0 'K3' 61857
	Brush Type 2 D5656
Saturday 4 August	2-6-0 'K3' 61875, 61889

London, which passed through mid-afternoon, and from the 'Birdcage' I watched her go by on Tuesday 2 August hauled by 'Britannia' No 70028 *Royal Star*. The following Saturday 'Jubilee' No 45712 *Victory* and another 'Scot', No 46144 *Honourable Artillery Company*, were recorded passing through on trains, and March shed's 'Brit' No 70012 *John of Gaunt* was spotted outside the roundhouse at 15C.

With the summer evenings now with us, and my George Evans racing bike now fully repaired, I was enjoying meeting up with our crowd down at the Great Central, which by now included some young ladies who were turning up regularly to socialise with us. I remember some even smoked, and looked very grown up. Around this time we also discovered the 'Chuckie Inn' on Hinckley Road – not a pub but a food outlet that opened late into the evening. For me and some of the boys it was on the way home after we had seen the evening's 'Fish', so we soon became regulars, calling in for a burger or faggot and peas for supper. Very soon it became one of the fashionable places for us youngsters to hang around, and very importantly to be seen, with groups of us of the same age meeting up outside the premises.

August 1962 turned out to be a very special time for me; I was enjoying my hobby enormously, cramming in lots of trainspotting, including a couple of great days on the East Coast Main Line at Peterborough. On both occasions I went on my own. The first trip was on the Summer Bank Holiday, Monday 6 August, which turned out to be the only time I ever travelled from Leicester London Road station via Market Harborough to my destination. Why was it special? Well, during my time there I took some photographs, a couple of which turned out to be my all-time favourites. Having arrived at the North station, I decided to walk the mile and an half to New England shed (34E), stopping en route to purchase a morning newspaper, whose headline shocked me by reporting 'Film Star Marilyn Monroe Found Dead'. Now, I don't know why but for some reason this particular headline has stayed with me over the years, so much so that I've never forgotten the date she tragically died or my trainspotting that day at Peterborough.

Despite being a Bank Holiday it proved to be a very busy day, during which I also managed to travel to March again. Starting at New England, I was able to wander around unchallenged, finding nearly a hundred locomotives on shed, with 25 'Austerities', 17 9Fs and 13 'V2s' and 'B1s'. Moving on to

I'm particularly fond of these two pictures, taken on that day. The first is of 'Britannia' No 70038 *Robin Hood* of Immingham shed (40B) just pulling away from the station that morning under the Crescent Bridge after stopping with Hull to King's Cross service.

In the second, Gresley 'A4' No 60008 *Dwight D. Eisenhower* pauses with a southbound Leeds to London express.

March, it was noticeable that the diesel depot area of 31B was now more established, with 21 Brush Type 2s present. Despite this, the steam shed was still busy with nine of its 'Brits' on view, together with 14 'B1s' to raise my spirits. I enjoyed a great day out with the added bonus of copping 'A3' 'Pacific' No 60036 *Colombo*, together with 'Brit' *Robin Hood*, which I photographed, and another, No 70007 *Coeur-de-Lion*, observed at March. It was also nice to see the summer 'Elizabethan' express pass through, even though it was now 'Deltic'-hauled, with newly named No D9012 *Crepello*

in charge, which I also 'copped'. I was very pleased to see another titled train, the 'Norseman', steam-hauled with 'A4' No 60028 *Walter K. Whigham* in charge, and a special hauled by the famous 'A3' No 60103 *Flying Scotsman*.

The very next day I was off again, this time with my family and my old school friend Big Stu on a day trip by train from the Great Central station to Leicester's favourite seaside destination, Skegness. Of course we still trainspotted, but there was a diversion. Her name was Sylvia, she was about 16 and lived a few doors away from me, and as our Mums were close friends she and her family joined us for the day out to the East Coast.

Now, to be honest I'd grown up living close to Sylvia without taking too much notice of her, but all of a sudden she became very pretty and grown up, to such an extent that both Stu and I fell in love. Now love does strange things to you, especially when you know that your friend had become a rival for the young lady's affections, and I spent the day doing my utmost to impress her, trying to be very grown-up and sophisticated, and even paying for her rides at the funfair. Sadly my advances came to nothing, and she managed to break both our hearts on the return journey when somehow she preferred an older boy, a bit greasy with a leather jacket, eventually leaving us and going off with him into another train compartment and pulling the blinds down. Were we jealous? Yes!

Our journey to the seaside town that day saw us hauled to Nottingham Victoria by 'Black 5' No 44847, where she was replaced by 'B1' No 61088 for the rest of the journey. A similar arrangement with the same engines occurred on the return journey, which saw us arrive back in Leicester close to midnight, where, despite there being no normal public service at that time, a fleet of Corporation buses was waiting to enable the passengers, including us, to get home around the city.

At least I had my hobby once more to console me, with a rare 'cop' of 'Brit' No 70020 *Mercury* down at the Midland the following day. Also on shed were a couple of 'Jubilees', Nos 45650 *Blake* and 45669 *Fisher*. Returning to my record book for further local spotting that August, I came across the title 'Paper Round', which was a nice reminder that I was still doing my evening delivery job, and with it came the perk of occasional sightings of trains on the former Great Central main line, which I could see running behind houses in the Blackbird Road area. There I saw 9F No 92087 two days running, together with a couple of English Electric Type 3 diesels, Nos D6744 and D6745.

My second visit to Peterborough was on Saturday 18 August, but on this occasion I changed my routine, deciding not to visit New England shed, nor travel to March, but to concentrate solely on the railway traffic that passed through the North station. To set the scene, I'm glad to say that despite the 'Deltics' now being in control of the line's principal expresses, and other classes of diesels appearing regularly, there was still a decent balance of steam express power hauling trains on a regular basis. I didn't mind a couple of trains in succession being diesel-hauled, because I knew there was a good chance that the next one would produce an 'A3' or 'A4', not forgetting one of the 'A1' or 'A2' 'Pacifics'. Little did I realise then that the day would turn out to be the last time I would witness my steam heroes hauling their famous East Coast expresses in any number. To be fair, my false sense of security with steam that August could be explained, because few of the region's express locomotives had been withdrawn despite the diesels, and all of my favourites, particularly the 'A4s', were still in service and, when seen working alongside other 'Pacifics', appeared to be in fine mechanical order, clean and well looked-after. On this particular day I was also trying to be a very grown-up trainspotter. True, I was still engine number recording, but trying to add a little bit more information about the trains I observed, all of which now helps to bring back the day's activity so vividly to me.

I can't help but think, looking back, that given the opportunity to relive one day from my railway enthusiast's adventures, this particular sunny one at Peterborough in August 1962 would certainly be one of my favourites. Despite the diesel invasion, and all the talk about modernisation, the day even managed to produce some old 4F 0-6-0 freight engines pressed into service on passenger specials, travelling from the Midlands to the East

Coast and passing through the North station before joining the old Midland & Great Northern main line to Hunstanton, Cromer and Yarmouth.

I was indeed enjoying myself, but of course I was growing up then with so few responsibilities and, as is often said, life seemed so much simpler then, as were our expectations, hence the packed holiday trains I witnessed. It's hard now to imagine now just how popular these holiday trains were, with the East Coast route even bestowing express status on them, with both the 'Scarborough Flyer' and the 'Filey Holiday Express' being blessed with 'Pacific' haulage that day. I wonder how many of those London holidaymakers, looking forward with their families to a week away at the seaside at Butlins Holiday Camp at Filey, realised that the legendry 'A4' 'Pacific' No 60022 *Mallard*, the fastest steam locomotive in the world, was hauling their train!

Peterborough trip, Saturday 18 August 1962		
Class	**Number/Name**	**Train**
Leicester station		
2-6-2T Class 2	41225, 41279	
2-8-0 8F	48384, 48380, 48197	
4-6-0 BR Class 4	75042	Local train
4-6-0 Br Class 4	75061	Local train
4-6-0 'Jubilee'	45611 *Hong Kong*	Special train
BR Type 4	D161	Nottingham-London
2-10-0 BR 9F	92157	
Leicester shed (15C)		
Class	**Number/Name**	
4-6-0 'Royal Scot'	46144 *The Honourable Artillery Company*	
BR Type 4	D116	

4-6-2 'A1' 60120 *Kittiwake* at Peterborough North. *Malcolm Castledine*

Leicester to Peterborough	
BR Type 4	D82 (pulled by)

Peterborough North station		
Class	**Number/Name**	**Train**
Brush Type 2	D5683	Special train
4-6-2 'A1'	60113 *Great Northern*	Anglo-Scottish car-carrier
EE Type 5	D9000 *Royal Scots Grey*	'West Riding Express',
Diesel shunters	D2240, D3487, D3445, D3630, D3488, No 81	
2-6-2 'V2'	60817	(later replaced failed 'Deltic')
4-6-0 'B1'	61179	Butlins Holiday Camp express
4-6-2 'A4'	60022 *Mallard*	Filey Holiday Express

Class	Number/Name	Train
EE Type 4	D247	London King's Cross-Edinburgh (special)
0-6-0 4F	44403	East Coast special
0-6-2T 'N2'	69579	(station shunter)
EE Type 4	D387	'White Rose', 10.30am
2-10-0 BR 9F	92037	Freight train
4-6-2 'A4'	60010 Dominion of Canada	London King's Cross-Edinburgh
4-6-2 'A1'	60118 Archibald Sturrock	Leeds-London King's Cross
4-6-2 'A3'	60105 Victor Wild	London King's Cross-Bradford
4-6-0 'B1'	61075	Skegness special
4-6-2 'Britannia'	70011 Hotspur	Peterborough-Leicester
EE Type 4	D388	Darlington-London King's Cross
0-6-0 4F	43969	East Coast special
EE Type 5	D9003 Meld	'Norseman', 10.55am
4-6-0 'B1'	61159	Skegness-London King's Cross
4-6-0 'B1'	61171	Local train
4-6-2 'A4'	60032 Gannet	London King's Cross-Newcastle, 11.05am
2-10-0 BR.9F	92036	Freight train
4-6-0 BR Class 4	75056	Leicester-Peterborough
4-6-2 'A2'	60523 Sun Castle	Special to Edinburgh
4-6-2 'A4'	60025 Falcon	Special to Bradford

Peterborough North station continued

4-6-2 'A4'	60110 *Robert the Devil*	Light engine
4-6-2 'A3'	60061 *Pretty Polly*	Special train
EE Type 5	D9011	'Flying Scotsman', 11.20am
4-6-0 'B1'	61059	Special train
4-6-2 'A4'	60003 *Andrew K. McCosh*	Durham-London King's Cross
Brush Type 2	D5611	Special train
EE Type 5	D9013 *The Black Watch*	Special train
EE Type 5	D9016	London King's Cross-Leeds
4-6-0 'B1'	61325	Local train
2-6-2 'V2'	60862	London King's Cross-Scarborough, 11.50am
4-6-0 Class 5	44966	Special train
4-6-2 'A1'	60121 *Silurian*	Hull-London King's Cross
2-6-2 'V2'	60938	Special train
4-6-0 BR Class 5	73000	Special train
4-6-2 'Britannia'	70038 *Robin Hood*	Cleethorpes-London King's Cross
4-6-2 'A4'	60034 *Lord Faringdon*	Special train
EE Type 5	D9020 *Nimbus*	London King's Cross-Glasgow, 12.30pm
EE Type 5	D9002	Special train
4-6-2 'A4'	60017 *Silver Fox*	Local train (footplate visit)
4-6-0 'B1'	61174	Special train
0-6-0 4F	44403	Special train

Class	Number/Name	Train
4-6-2 'A3'	60048 *Doncaster*	'Scarborough Flyer', 12.50pm
4-6-2 'A3'	60111 *Enterprise*	Special train
4-6-2 'A3'	60047 *Donovan*	Failed on London King's Cross-Newcastle
4-6-2 'A3'	60065 *Knight of Thistle*	Replaced 60047
Brush Type 2	D5683	Special train
0-6-2T 'N2' 3	69593	(station shunter)
4-6-0 Class 5	44772	Special train
2-6-2 'V2'	60966	Peterborough-London King's Cross
2-6-2 'V2'	60983	Local train
EE Type 5	D9004	'Queen of Scots' Pullman, 1.24pm
4-6-2 'A3'	60088 *Book Law*	Newcastle-London King's Cross
4-6-2 'A1'	60119 *Patrick Stirling*	London King's Cross-Hull
EE Type 5	D9014	Newcastle-London King's Cross
0-6-0 4F	44403 and 43969	Together hauling a special train
EE Type 4	D272	Freight train
EE Type 4	D354	London King's Cross-York
4-6-2 'A1'	60120 *Kittiwake*	'Yorkshire Pullman'
2-6-2 'V2'	60862	Peterborough-London King's Cross
EE Type 5	D9014	'Northumbrian' (failed)

A 'Deltic' approaches Peterborough North from the south, passing Crescent Junction. *Tony Moore*

2-6-2 'V2'	60817	Replaced failed 'Deltic'
4-6-0 'B1'	61179	Butlins Holiday Express
4-6-2 'A3'	60109 *Hermit*	'Scarborough Flyer', 1.56pm
4-6-2 'A3'	60103 *Flying Scotsman*	Special train
Brush Type 2	D5614	London King's Cross-Leeds
4-6-0 'B1'	61366	Skegness-Peterborough
EE Type 4	D281	London King's Cross-Newcastle, 2.25pm
4-6-0 Class 5	44816	Special train
2-6-2 'V2'	60983	Local train
BR Type 4	D62	Leicester-Peterborough
4-6-2 'A1'	60122 *Curlew*	London King's Cross-Leeds

Class	Number/Name	Train
2-8-0 'WD'	90502	Freight train
4-6-2 'A3'	60039 *Sandwich*	Special train
4-6-0 'B1'	61073	Butlins Holiday Express, 2.47pm
4-6-0 'B1'	61366	Light engine
EE Type 5	D9008	Edinburgh-London King's Cross
EE Type 5	D9000 *Royal Scots Grey*	Relief 'Flying Scotsman'
4-6-2 'A3' 6	0049 *Galtee More*	London King's Cross-Bradford
EE Type 5	D9009 *Alycidon*	'Flying Scotsman', 3.00pm
4-6-2 'A3'	60067 *Ladas*	Special train
2-10-0 BR 9F	92041	Freight train
EE Type 4	D387	'Heart of Midlothian'
4-6-0 'B1'	61394	Light engine
2-6-2 'V2'	60880	Light engine
4-6-2 'A3'	60066 *Merry Hampton*	Leeds-London King's Cross
4-6-2 'A3'	60046 *Diamond Jubilee*	London King's Cross-York, 3.34pm
BR Type 4	D62	Peterborough-Leicester
4-6-2 'A4'	60022 *Mallard*	Filey Holiday Camp Express
4-6-0 'B1'	61074	London King's Cross-Cleethorpes
2-8-0 'WD'	90130	Freight train
0-6-0 4F	44013	Special train

EE Type 4	D392	
Brush Type 2	D5611	Hauling failed 'Deltic' D9014
Brush Type 2	D5608	Freight train
4-6-2 'A1'	60139 Sea Eagle	London King's Cross-Bradford, 4.30pm
Brush Type 2	D5602	
4-6-0 'B1'	61171	Light engine
BR Type 4	D174	Special train
EE Type 4	D395	'Norseman'
EE Type 4	D240	Special train
0-6-0 4F	43876	Special train
4-6-2 'A2'	60526 Sugar Palm	Light engine
EE Type 4	D393	Newcastle-London King's Cross
4-6-2 'A2'	60523 Sun Castle	Light engine
EE Type 5	D9018 Ballymoss	Newcastle-London King's Cross
4-6-0 Class 5	44777	Special train
EE Type 4	D388	London King's Cross-York
4-6-2 'A4'	60014 Silver Link	'Northumbrian'
4-6-2 'A1'	60123 H. A. Ivatt	London King's Cross-Leeds, 4.56pm
4-6-2 'A4'	60034 Lord Faringdon	York- London King's Cross
4-6-2 'A2'	60513 Dante	Special train
4-6-2 'A4'	60003 Andrew K. McCosh	Freight train
2-10-0 BR 9F	92044	Freight train

Peterborough North station continued		
Class	**Number/Name**	**Train**
4-6-0 'B1'	61406	Local train
4-6-2 'Britannia'	70038 *Robin Hood*	London King's Cross-Cleethorpes
Brush Type 2	D5639	Freight train
4-6-2 'A4'	60017 *Silver Fox*	'White Rose'
4-6-2 'A1'	60121 *Silurian*	London King's Cross-Leeds, 5.16pm
4-6-2 'A4'	60013 *Dominion of Canada*	London King's Cross-York
4-6-0 BR Class 4	75060	Pulled by, Peterborough-Leicester

Leicester shed (15C)	
Class	**Number/Name**
4-6-0 'Royal Scot'	46130 *The West Yorkshire Regiment*
BR Type 4	D163

Mentioning 'A4s', the day was also to provide me with a wonderful memory of being allowed up onto the footplate of No 60017 *Silver Fox*, where I was stunned to find that the footplate crew had red leather bucket seats, a comfort I'd never seen before in a steam locomotive cab, and to be told by the proud driver that, despite the introduction of the 'Deltics', his engine was still capable of 100mph running.

Now, being a teenager in the 'Swinging Sixties' trying to impress the ever-growing band of youngsters meeting up down the Great Central line, I soon realised that trainspotting didn't attract the kind of interest among our female visitors that I was hoping for, so overnight I became a pop music fan, and thus able to enter into meaningful discussions about the latest stars featured on Radio Luxemburg, including Brenda Lee, Chubby Checker, Cliff Richard and the Shadows, and a very young Helen Shapiro. Some of the other lads even started to bring their 45rpm vinyl records to swap and lend to each other, so not wishing to be left out that August I went and bought my first ever record, *Sealed with a Kiss* by Brian Hyland. The only problem I had, to which I never admitted, was that I couldn't play it, because at home we didn't have a record player; my parents were happy with their radio, and the popular model of the time, the 'Dansette', cost around £11, so was viewed as a luxury, so certainly not a priority in our household. Now, before you feel too sorry for me, I'll jump ahead another 12 months when, thanks to earning a regular wage I was able to purchase the very latest three-speed version thanks to a new financial idea called 'hire purchase', and my bedroom was soon rocking with all the latest hits.

The Wednesday after my trip to Peterborough I was off on a visit to Crewe Works, this time on a special train with Big Stu, who was on holiday from work. I haven't a clue who organised the excursion, as it was advertised in the our local *Mercury* newspaper, which was unusual, as was our train's route to Crewe, because instead of travelling the normal route through Derby, we actually travelled along the Burton-on-Trent branch via Desford, Coalville, Ashby-de-la-Zouch and Gresley to Burton, a line that was to see its passenger traffic withdrawn in 1964. Another surprise came when we arriving at the Midland station and found the special being hauled by what we enthusiasts described as a 'double header' – two steam engines coupled together – both of which, 4F No 44403 and 'Black 5' No 44815, were Leicester-based locomotives.

Departing from London Road, we soon passed high along the embankment on the Burton line overlooking the Great Central shed and saw 'V2' No 60815, which sadly had been withdrawn in April and was standing in the yard awaiting its fate. Likewise two Johnson 2Fs, Nos 58166 and 58305, were in store at Coalville, although sister engines Nos 58138 and 58143 were in steam and in service.

Arriving at Burton, our 4F, No 44403, was taken off the train, and we continued our journey with No 44815 in sole charge, passing through Uttoxeter where we saw ex-works 9F No 92211 on shed. On to the Potteries, and a haul of numbers was obtained as we passed Stoke shed (5D) yard, including five 2-6-0 'Crab' engines, one of which, No 42888, was a welcome 'cop' for me.

Now I'm fairly certain that when our special train arrived at Crewe we slowly passed through the station without stopping and pulled into the actual works area, because we certainly passed Crewe North shed (5A), which reminds me of the following concern. Looking back at my records that day I came across an uncomfortable 'cop' for me of Scottish-based 'Royal Scot' No 46105 *Cameron Highlander*. Why uncomfortable? Well, it was one of those occasions when we were travelling by a locomotive shed, and yours truly was scribbling down the engine numbers as fast as I could while someone else was shouting them out. This was the usual way of trying to record the most numbers possible when passing often crowded shed yards, with lines of locomotives on view. On trainspotters' specials, as we were in this case, you can imagine the noise created with numbers of different engines being shouting out in quick succession from all directions. It only took a second or so, but when *Cameron*'s number was called out, as she was one of the few 'Scots' I still needed I quickly glanced across to the North's shed yard, and sure enough I could see a 'Royal Scot' in the distance, but her number was by then a blur. To be fair, the other lads were adamant it was her, so into my Ian Allan *abc* 'Combine' she was underlined as seen, but was it really her? I sincerely hope so, because I was never able to see her again.

My overwhelming memory of our visit to the works that day was the sight of the famous 'Princess Coronation' engine No 46220 *Coronation* standing in the Paint Shop fresh from overhaul and looking stunning in her newly applied shining green livery. This particular locomotive, the doyen of the class, had proved difficult for me to track down over the years, with very few observations of her working, so it was a real surprise to find her

Crewe North (5A), shed yard	
Class	**Number/Name**
2-6-2T Class 2	41201, 41220
4-6-0 Class 5	45344
EE Type 4	D210 *Empress of Britain*, D236, D327
4-6-0 'Royal Scot'	46105 *Cameron Highlander*, 46138 *The London Irish Rifleman*, 46167 *The Hertfordshire Regiment*
4-6-2 'Princess Coronation'	46229 *Duchess of Hamilton*
BR Type 4 'Warship'	D805 *Benbow*, D815 *Druid*
BR Type 4 'Western'	D1037 *Western Empress* (new build)
Electric locos	E3020, E3100, E3017, E3005
4-6-2 'Britannia'	70020 *Mercury*
4-6-0 'Jubilee'	45557 *New Brunswick*
0-6-0 4F	43957
0-6-0T 3F	47658

there, and even more reason to enjoy studying her close up. I'm sure one of my hobby's attractions was the size of these express engines; she truly was a massive engine, both in size and power. No wonder her class of 'Pacifics' stood alongside the Gresley 'A4s' way on top of my list of 'steam heroes'.

Looking around, it was nice to see the works still busy with steam loco repairs, and I was pleased to come across a couple of North Eastern Region 2-6-0 BR Standards, Nos 77001 and 77004, together with 'Jubilee' No 45600 *Bermuda*, which was receiving attention in the Repair Shop, all of which I 'copped'.

At this time Crewe Works was heavily engaged in building the new generation of diesel locomotives for British Railways, but what I didn't anticipate was that Crewe, as well as Swindon, would be involved in the construction of diesel-hydraulics for the

Western Region; we saw all but the first of the batch being built there in 1962, Nos D1035-D1053.

Our journey home, once again hauled by No 44815, saw most of us checking the numbers collected to see what 'cops' we had got, with one or two lads bragging that they had cleared their 'Scots' or 'Brits' for a bit of one-upmanship. My journey wasn't so pleasant as, having consumed a couple of Hayes's fruit pies and a couple of bars of Fry's 5 Centre Chocolate Cream, plus crisps washed down by swigs of cider, I was poorly. Thankfully I was saved by the 'Black Watch'. No, not the rare 'Royal Scot' loco, but Big Stu's black and green tartan duffel bag, in which I deposited the insides of my tummy. My best friend was not my best friend for a few days afterwards, but at least his precious *abc* was in his pocket not in the bag, and I did spend 12s 6d buying him a new bag the following week.

Three days later, fully recovered, I was off again, this time to yet another railway works, to Derby, returning once more for the annual Open Day. This time, however, my visit didn't pass without incident, because on the train journey home one of our friends managed to get himself in trouble with the Transport Police. This lad, whom I had met through the Great Central Railway Society, had joined a few of us in our compartment as we travelled back after the works visit on the 'Palatine' express to Leicester. We were all having a laugh and some leg-pulling as we were speeding along when Pete suddenly got up and started to unscrew some of the carriage light bulbs above our seats, and threw them out of the compartment's upper sliding windows, smashing them on the track. It was all a bit sudden, and we were taken back at what he had done, because it was completely out of character for him. Thankfully the rest of us had the good sense not to join in, because a few minutes later the doors of our compartment burst open and in came a uniformed Railway Transport Policeman demanded to know who had thrown the light bulbs onto the track. We were all shocked and scared, but thankfully Pete quickly owned up and was hauled away to make a statement; we all counted ourselves very lucky that we hadn't been involved.

A few months later, long after I'd forgotten about the incident,

I was astonished to pick up our local evening paper, the *Mercury*, and read on its front page 'Youth fined for Train Vandalism'. Sure enough, it was Pete who found himself in front of the City Magistrates for his moment of madness, and was subsequently heavily fined. Looking back, for his offence to warrant such publicity seems completely over the top and certainly didn't warrant front-page news, but there you go. The repercussions for him must have been awful and certainly ended his trainspotting hobby, as we never saw him again, which was a pity.

I'm sorry to talk about diesels first, but three of the pioneers were noted at the works that day: 1947 Derby-built Co-Co engine No 10001, and two of the early-1950s Southern Region 1Co-Co1s, Nos 10201 and 10203. While on the subject of diesels, in the Erecting Shop were no fewer than 13 members of the 'Peak' Class under construction. Steam was still being repaired, with six BR Standard Class 5s found in the Repair Shop, one of which, No 73167, was a 'cop' for me, together with Stanier tank engine No 42500, which, although on the scrap line, was eventually to be preserved.

We then made the fateful journey back to Leicester on the 'Palatine' hauled by a 'Peak' D51. Arriving back at Leicester, 'Britannia' 'Pacific' No 70003 *Geoffrey Chaucer* was noted in the

Derby Works Open Day, Saturday 25 August 1962	
Class	**Number/Name**
Locomotives on display:	
4-6-2 'Princess Coronation'	46256 *Sir William A. Stanier F.R.S.*
4-6-2 'Britannia'	70048 *The Territorial Army 1908-1958*
BR Type 4	D178 (new)
Diesel shunters	D2378, D2380
Midland 'Compound'	1000
2-6-4T Class 4	42146, 42184
Preserved steam engines	158A, 118, 80 *Thundersley*

Locomotives on display at Derby Works Open Day, 1962. *Tony Moore* yard at 15C, together with English Electric diesel No D341.

Rounding off our local interest in August, a visit to the Central the following Thursday saw me collect three steam 'cops', Western Region visitor 'Hall' No 6970 *Whaddon Hall* and two 'K3s', Nos 61819 and 61952.

September started well, but it wasn't to last; as indicated by my records that month, my trainspotting visits slowed down when I started full-time employment on the 10th. But the implications of that momentous day and its effects on my trainspotting will have to wait until volume 2...